IRIS MURDOCH'S ETHICS

Continuum Studies in British Philosophy
Series Editor: James Fieser, University of Tennessee at Martin, USA

Continuum Studies in British Philosophy is a major monograph series from Continuum. The series features first-class scholarly research monographs across the field of Continental philosophy. Each work makes a major contribution to the field of philosophical research.

Applying Wittgenstein – Rupert Read
Berkeley and Irish Philosophy – David Berman
Berkeley's Philosophy of Spirit – Talia Bettcher
Bertrand Russell, Language and Linguistic Theory – Keith Green
Bertrand Russell's Ethics – Michael K. Potter
Boyle on Fire – William Eaton
The Coherence of Hobbes's Leviathan – Eric Brandon
Doint Austin Justice – Wilfrid Rumble
The Early Wittgenstein on Religion – J. Mark Lazenby
F.P. Ramsey, edited by Maria J. Frapolli
Francis Bacon and the Limits of Scientific Knowledge – Dennis Desroches
Hume's Social Philosophy – Christopher Finlay
Hume's Theory of Causation – Angela Coventry
Idealist Political Philosophy – Colin Tyler
Iris Murdoch's Ethics – Megan Lavery
John Stuart Mill's Political Philosophy – John Fitzpatrick
Matthew Tindal, Freethinker – Stephen Lalor
The Philosophy of Herbert Spencer – Michael Taylor
Popper, Objectivity and the Growth of Knowledge – John H. Sceski
Rethinking Mill's Ethics – Colin Heydt
Russell's Theory of Perception – Sajahan Miah
Russell and Wittgenstein on the Nature of Judgement – Rosalind Carey
Thomas Hobbes and the Politics of Natural Philosophy – Stephen J. Finn
Thomas Reid's Ethics – William C. Davis
Wittgenstein and Gadamer – Chris Lawn
Wittgenstein and the Theory of Perception – Justin Good
Wittgenstein at his Word – Duncan Richter
Wittgenstein on Ethical Inquiry – Jeremy Wisnewski
Wittgenstein's Religious Point of View – Tim Labron

IRIS MURDOCH'S ETHICS
A Consideration of her Romantic Vision

MEGAN LAVERTY

continuum

Continuum International Publishing Group
The Tower Building, 11 York Road, London SE1 7NX
80 Maiden Lane, Suite 704, New York, NY 10038
www.continuumbooks.com

© Megan Laverty 2007

All rights reserved. No part of this publication may be reproduced or transmitted in any form or by any means, electronic or mechanical, including photocopying, recording, or any information storage or retrieval system, without prior permission in writing from the publishers.

British Library Cataloguing-in-Publication Data
A catalogue record for this book is available from the British Library.

ISBN: HB: 0-8264-8535-9
978-0-8264-8535-9

Library of Congress Cataloguing-in-Publication Data
Laverty, Megan.
  Iris Murdoch's ethics : a consideration of her romantic vision / Megan Laverty.
    p. cm.
  ISBN-13: 978-0-8264-8535-9
  ISBN-10: 0-8264-8535-9
  1. Murdoch, Iris. 2. Ethics. I. Title.

BJ604.M873L38 2007
170.92–dc22

2007011189

Typeset by Aarontype Limited, Easton, Bristol
Printed and bound in Great Britain by Biddles Ltd, King's Lynn, Norfolk

For my daughter, Elizabeth

Contents

Abbreviations	viii
Acknowledgements	x
Introduction	1
1 A Philosophy of the 'Third Way'	17
2 Reading Murdoch: Literary Form and Philosophical Precedents	37
3 Romanticism Reconsidered	58
4 Resistance and Reconciliation	73
5 Murdoch's Romantic Vision	91
Notes	110
Bibliography	123
Index	131

Abbreviations

EM Peter Conradi (ed.), *Existentialists and Mystics: Writings on Philosophy and Literature* (New York: Penguin Books, 1997).
MGM Iris Murdoch, *Metaphysics as a Guide to Morals* (London: Chatto & Windus, 1992).
SG Iris Murdoch, *The Sovereignty of Good* (London: Routledge & Kegan Paul, 1970).
SRR Iris Murdoch, *Sartre: Romantic Rationalist* (London: Penguin, 1953).

The gift of leaving
Is to slip somewhere silent or sacred
In the repossessed spells of the old ways,
The shadow of my voice, fall of my step,
So that bound by what is left behind,
Returning is assured, like all things unknown.
                              (Robyn Rowland)

I have been away a long time,
Forgotten just how quiet it can seem.
No Penelope, no good blind Argos chivied by fleas.
No suitors to slay.
How terribly long its takes:
The books and closets and outside plants
Finding their ways back into one's head,
Where and in what order.
Away for so long I'm other than I was,
Having again to learn simply how to be here,
As if having another go at the piano
After how many years.
                              (August Kleinzahler)

Acknowledgements

Iris Murdoch writes that 'repentance may mean something different to an individual at different times in his life, and what it fully means is part of this life and cannot be understood except in context' (*SG*, p. 26). The same can be said of my understanding of her moral philosophy: the story of this book is in many respects the story of my life. Its gradual gestation owes a lot to a great many people and I regret that I cannot record everyone by name. I have benefited as much from the disparate array of miscellaneous people in my life as I have from my readings of, and conversations with, some of the finest scholars on Murdoch and German philosophy, including Karl Ameriks, Maria Antonaccio, Marcia Baron and Lawrence Blum.

My first debt of gratitude is to Christopher Cordner for introducing me to Murdoch's moral philosophy and for encouraging me to pursue my interest in her; although this book is a far cry from my earliest writings on Murdoch's moral philosophy it remains, I hope, very much in the spirit nurtured by those early conversations. My next debt of gratitude is to the inimitable Genevieve Lloyd, who patiently, and with bemused puzzlement I suspect, shaped my interest in Murdoch's moral philosophy and its relationship to both Wittgensteinian moral philosophy and romanticism. She managed to enlarge my awareness from what I was trying to say to the philosophical implications of my readings. If philosophy is being able to stand back from what one is, does or thinks to reflect on it, then Genevieve Lloyd embodies that endeavour. I return time and time again to her incandescent philosophical writings.

There have been others who have had an important role in my development as an academic philosopher and, as a consequence, the gestation of this book. Raimond Gaita's moral philosophy remains an important resource for my reflections on moral philosophy, and I am grateful for the support that he has shown me over the years. Brian Scarlett was instrumental in my first academic position and always made me feel welcome at the department 'watering-hole'. Tony Coady has always been there to lift my spirits and provide astute and expert advice. Marcia Baron has offered warm and collegial support over the years. Teresa Brennan treated me as a peer and friend early on in my philosophy graduate studies. John Ozolins and Peter Drum included me in the philosophical community at the Australian Catholic University. My close friend Diana Barnes continues to read my writing. Peter Dlugos exemplifies the true spirit of philosophical friendship — I am grateful for his concern and care as well as for our many searching and illuminating conversations together; his humour, honesty, humility and wisdom continue to inspire my work in professional philosophy. Jeremy Moss continues to be a friend and colleague and has not lost his sense of humour. Sarah Redshaw has encouraged me to persevere, as she has persevered herself. Dorothy Rogers kindly introduced me to my publisher, Continuum, and also to the early American thinker Kate Gordon Moore.

I want particularly to thank Ann Margaret Sharp, Matthew Lipman, Philip Guin, Maughn Gregory, David Kennedy and Mark Weinstein of the Institute for the Advancement of Philosophy for Children (IAPC) at Montclair State University, for their openness, joy and ongoing philosophical activism. I feel honoured to be part of their community. I am delighted to be able to thank David Hansen for taking me seriously as a scholar and for sharing my appreciation of Murdoch's educational importance. I am grateful to him for giving me the opportunity to pursue my research on Murdoch's moral philosophy and for allowing me to share in his philosophical and pedagogical wisdom. Working with him is and, continues to be, a pleasure.

My greatest and most complicated debt is to Laurance Splitter. Over the last fifteen years he has been friend, confidant, mentor, teacher, colleague, critic and editor. He is a remarkably generous person. So, although not a moral philosopher, and largely sceptical about Murdoch's moral philosophy, he has persistently and patiently listened to me speak about her and has read numerous drafts of my papers. I know that he does this in the spirit of friendship and his sincere hope that formal education might be organized around values of cooperation, mutual respect and concern for one another. I am grateful to him for all that he has shared with me.

Since coming to Teachers College in 2005 I have benefited from the conscientious research assistance of doctoral students Mark Jonas and Rodino Anderson. I owe a debt of gratitude to my friends Pablo Cevallos Estarellas and Norma Zulardi for their expert editorial advice, as I have learned a great deal about writing from both of them. I would like to thank Philip De Bary, formerly of Continuum, for commissioning this book on Iris Murdoch, and Sarah Douglas for her patience and support in overseeing it in its final stages.

The material in these chapters on Iris Murdoch and philosophical romanticism has been presented in a number of different scholarly forums in a variety of forms. In 2006 I gave a public lecture on Iris Murdoch for the

Women's History Month at Bergen Community College. In 2004 I presented my work on Iris Murdoch to a panel at the International Association for Philosophy and Literature (IAPL) conference and to the Philosophy department of Mount Holyoke College. In 2006 I gave an invited presentation on Iris Murdoch to an international conference on ethics education in Korea. I would like to thank the individuals present on these occasions for their comments and words of encouragement, in particular Marije Altorf, Jin Whan Park and Thomas Wartenburg. In 2003 I first introduced the notion of romantic ethics as part of the annual Phenomenology and Literature Conference. My paper, 'The interplay of virtue and romantic ethics in Chang rae Lee's *A Gesture Life*' was later published in *Analecta Husserliana*, 85 (ed. A.T. Tymieniecka).

There are two smaller forums that I wish to acknowledge: the Philosophy and Education Colloquia at Teachers College, Columbia University, and the annual Simone Weil Colloquium. I have regularly presented papers in these contexts to sympathetic but sophisticated and critical responses. I am particularly grateful to my engagements with Martin Andic, David Hansen and Eric Springsted.

The people mentioned so far have been scholars, teachers and colleagues. I want to thank those students who have allowed me to become a teacher by considering that I had something to teach. Ironically, more than anyone else, they have taught me how important it is both to trust our desires and articulate them. I would particularly like to thank Andrew Gaff and Mark Jonas in this regard.

Finally, none of this would have been possible, or have seemed as valuable, without the support of my neighbours and the love of my family and friends. They have endured the writing of this book. In *The Sovereignty of Good*, Murdoch writes that goodness is 'both rare and hard to picture' (p. 53). It is Brendan's goodness – his fidelity, patience and humour – that is the necessary, less visible, background to this book. Without him none of it would have been possible.

Introduction

Until recently, Dame Iris Murdoch has been studied as a novelist rather than as a moral philosopher; however, interest in her philosophy is now growing. Since 1996, several books on Murdoch's moral philosophy have appeared,[1] the number of articles on aspects of her philosophy has increased,[2] an Iris Murdoch society has been formed and the Centre for Iris Murdoch Studies opened in 2004.[3] Lastly, there is now an annual international conference devoted to philosophical aspects of Murdoch's writings.[4] With the mounting scholarship on Murdoch's philosophy, criticism of it is no longer 'at a naïve stage' (Dipple 1982, p. x) and claims that the significance of her philosophical thought is 'underappreciated' (Holland 1988, p. 181) by philosophers have become less valid.

The reasons for the initial neglect of Murdoch's moral philosophy are various. Some are historical. Although Murdoch continued to teach as a philosopher during most of her academic life, there is a gap of just over 20 years between the first publication of *The Sovereignty of Good* (*SG*, 1970) and her next book, *Metaphysics as a Guide to Morals* (*MGM*, 1992). Some are academic. Murdoch's prodigious success as a novelist eclipsed her early writings in philosophy, making her the 'property' of literary critics.[5] Some reasons are philosophical. The dominance of analytic philosophy within Anglo-American academia created an environment that was not receptive to alternative ways of engaging with philosophy. Other reasons are scholarly. With the exception of *The Sovereignty of Good*, Murdoch's philosophical writings were dispersed in different scholarly journals, only later to be brought together in a volume edited by Peter Conradi, *Existentialists and Mystics: Writings on Philosophy and Literature* (*EM*).

The reasons for the recent interest in Murdoch's philosophy are equally various. Some of them are historical. Murdoch succumbed to Alzheimer's disease in the latter part of her life. This was recorded by her husband, John Bayley, in his memoir of her (which was adapted into a film) (Bayley 1998; also 1999). This, combined with Peter Conradi's dedication to Murdoch as a thinker, writer and friend, has contributed to a surge of interest in her life and work. An extremely private person in life, Murdoch has become a public figure in death (Conradi 2001). Some reasons are academic. There is now a higher tolerance for interdisciplinary research; a deep suspicion of claims to universality, the emergence of historicism and materialist analysis; and a more complex psychology that acknowledges emotions and interpersonal relationships. Some reasons are philosophical. The community of professional philosophers has, by and large, caught up with Murdoch, due in large part to the developments of feminism and virtue ethics, as well as (perhaps more tangentially) postmodernism, and practical and applied philosophy.

The consensus is steadily building that Murdoch is a significant twentieth-century philosopher who is 'speaking directly to our [human] condition' (*EM*, p. xxxvii). If, as Conradi surmises, it was 'the madnesses of Europe' that 'hurt Iris Murdoch into moral philosophy', then perhaps it is 'the madnesses' of contemporary society that direct us now to Murdoch's moral philosophy with its 'urgent seriousness' and 'compassionate clear-sightedness' (*EM*, pp. xix, xvi). Irrespective of this claim's truth, Murdoch presides over many of the most significant contemporary developments within moral philosophy today. So although her philosophy has only recently become the subject of extensive philosophical study, her ideas are profoundly influential. They have been taken up by contemporary Wittgensteinian philosophers including, most notably, Cora Diamond (1991) and Raimond Gaita (1991), by moral particularists such as Lawrence Blum (1994) and Martha Nussbaum (1990), by moral realists such as John McDowell (1979), and by feminists writing in the domain of feminist ethics and an ethics of care like Sarah Ruddick (1995).

Motivated by a desire to do justice to Murdoch's genius, scholars such as Maria Antonaccio, Peta Bowden, Bran Nicol, Heather Widdows and others are examining and explicating Murdoch's philosophical and literary work.[6] The scholarship is dominated by exegetical questions because it is motivated by the desire to establish her place within the Western philosophical tradition. Scholars research Murdoch's texts according to broad preexisting conceptual frameworks – such as existentialism, Christian existentialism, Platonism, Christian Platonism, and metaphysical realism – in order to found philosophical credibility. This work endeavours to justify the scholarly philosophical attention that Murdoch's philosophy deserves by demonstrating its capacity to stand its own ground within these traditions. In this spirit, the following study articulates her philosophy within the tradition of philosophical romanticism – a term taken from Nikolas Kompridis (2006) – depicting the authority of her philosophy as given by its location in, and ability to comment on, a larger philosophical tradition, in this case romantic.[7]

Introduction 3

While it is true that a respectable evaluation of Murdoch's philosophy is going to rely on an unambiguous specification of it, such identification is complicated by the elusive and chameleon-like qualities of Murdoch's philosophy: her philosophical interests straddle both continental and analytical traditions, and her readings of the philosophical tradition are highly individual.[8] The 'objective' analysis of Murdoch's argument can, therefore, have the effect of silencing what is most distinctive about her philosophical voice. It becomes difficult to hear Murdoch's particular eloquence in the careful analysis of her arguments and terms; the quality of her philosophy that arrests attention and eludes immediate articulation tends to be lost, or, at least overshadowed, by the commentary. I argue that, of all the philosophical traditions, romanticism uniquely does justice to the enigmatic quality of Murdoch's work. Romanticism celebrates her anomalous status within Anglo-American professional philosophy and, as a consequence, offers a more complex and subtle interpretation of her philosophy.[9] For it is within the context of philosophical romanticism that Murdoch can be interpreted as reconciling, rather than confusing, the following set of concerns: the philosophical and poetic; synthesis and divergence as dialogical necessities; Kant's Copernican Revolution and Platonist metaphysics; existentialism and Platonism;[10] the artist and the saint; and, lastly, 'Socrates and the virtuous peasant' (*SG*, p. 2).

It is the resonance of Murdoch's philosophy with philosophical romanticism that highlights her deep appreciation for paradox as a necessary feature of the human condition and wisdom. To be wise, on Murdoch's view, is passionately to inhabit significant paradoxes of human existence, the most central of which is the simultaneous 'pointlessness' and 'unique value' of virtue (*SG*, p. 104). Rather than representing a position that individuals arrive at, wisdom reflects a deep immersion in, and understanding of, the experience of *learning*. It is practised, realized in relationship to the activities, experiences and relationships that typify learning. Learning is characterized by: an impulse to understand reality and the realization that understanding is finite; a desire for dialogical synthesis and the recognition of its undesirability; and a conclusive knowing combined with vulnerable susceptibility towards what exceeds knowledge.

Murdoch's philosophy is a call for humanity to embrace these paradoxes, and exercise our partial freedom within them, instead of being tempted to resolve them in the search for greater certainty and finality (freedom versus determinism, truth versus falsity and ignorance versus knowledge, for example). Murdoch's intent is entirely ethical. She believes that our ability to tolerate ambiguity makes justice and virtue possible. This is because individuals take a greater responsibility for consciousness (and not just deliberation) as they ground it in relational responses to experience (affective, habitual and somatic for example); individuals become more circumspect in their judgements and less egoistically invested in them; and individuals are more prepared to enter into dialogue with one another, accepting that it is impossible to know a priori what moral significance our similarities and differences will have.

My argument in this book is not historical. I am not suggesting that Murdoch's philosophy has its roots in or, is influenced by, European romanticism.[11] Nor am I suggesting that she claims, or ought to claim, an association with 'romanticism' – her position on this point remains ambivalent. Rather, my argument is hermeneutical and philosophical. I suggest that it is possible to think of Murdoch as engaging in a dialogue with analytic moral philosophy and philosophical romanticism, and that part of her purpose in explicitly targeting the arguments of analytic moral philosophy is to bring philosophical romanticism into the conversation. It is analogous to when, in the *Meno*, Socrates 'teaches' the slave-boy a lesson so as to illustrate a point and shame Meno into a more genuine and sustained enquiry; and when, in the *Gorgias*, Socrates engages Polus in conversation for its own sake, but also as a necessary first stage in a much longer conversation with Callicles. Murdoch is speaking to the concerns of philosophical romanticism as she speaks with analytic moral philosophers.

This is not just a formal point, for it produces an alternative interpretation of Murdoch's philosophy that I now summarize as a preface to the argument of the book. Murdoch's philosophy is premised on a version of Kant's Copernican Revolution: humans cannot directly know noumenal reality because our experience is necessarily phenomenal: that is, consciousness mediates and delimits human experience. Murdoch characterizes consciousness as imaginative; it pictures reality; it is whole-making and form-giving. Individuals perceive reality through lenses; tropes are repeated across 'different' encounters, giving experience uniformity and meaning. The range of possibilities is not that great because consciousness is governed by the psyche (more of this presently). Murdoch concludes that noumenal reality, constituted as the absence of consciousness, must be, by definition at least, formlessness; devoid of meaning and unity, reality is sheer nothingness. This nothingness – represented in Murdoch's philosophy by death, chance and void – is the reality that transcends consciousness and is so very difficult for us to acknowledge. Wherever you look, humans are prepared to accept just about any other position – solipsism, determinism, nihilism or existentialism even – so as to avoid acknowledging their lack of significance and differentiation.

The epistemic task for Murdoch, as it is for Kant, is to determine which of our experiences warrant the label 'objective'. Murdoch argues that the Copernican Revolution properly entails that there can be no discernible systematic criterion for objectivity. We are as humans, 'fallen': despite our best efforts we cannot definitively secure the true nature of objectivity or reality. It does not follow that we do not have a sense (flashes of insight, intuition, inkling, presentiment, intimation) of the direction in which objectivity and, ultimately, reality, resides. For, keeping in mind the formlessness of reality, anything which directs consciousness to both our human mortality and that, individuals are, as human beings, ultimately subject to chance (the most extreme of which is death) is pointing us in the right direction through its alignment of consciousness with reality.

Humans take on a special significance in this regard, for they commonly inspire 'readings' of reality that are in accordance with our desires. Murdoch loosely accepts that the patterns of individual consciousness are established in our earliest interactions in relationship to the desires that they establish and serve, such as thinking well or badly of oneself, rationalizing or catastrophizing failure, giving power over or seeking to dominate others. Yet humans are also representative of reality's dramatic refusal to conform to any, and all, projected meanings, for it is the case that individuals, including ourselves, feel, behave and change unpredictably and inexplicably. Other individuals are simultaneously the most and least difficult things to see clearly. The imperative to 'see truthfully' is most compelling in the case of other human beings because of their vulnerability and, because we are reliant on them to provide the necessary checks to our own consciousness – this can only occur if we resist assimilating them to the patterns of our consciousness.

It follows that Murdoch's philosophy relies on a revolutionized concept of the sublime. Premised on a version of the Kantian Copernican Revolution, her philosophy theorizes that most humans, most of the time, have experiences of the sublime – including individuals that least deserve it. The sublime is any experience which induces learning. Learning, as Murdoch defines it, occurs when an individual comes up against a limit to her conceptual understanding. Murdoch assumes, at this point, that the discernment of a limit implies the creation of new, yet-to-be-discovered limits, because to demarcate a limit is, in some inchoate sense, to see beyond it to the other side, that is, to detect what conceptual understanding could be like. Hence, Murdoch defines the sublime as a pedagogical encounter with the limits of imaginative consciousness; it initiates a conceptual transformation within the individual as she struggles to articulate its felt significance – in some cases discovering new meanings for old words, or finding new words, both of which are reflected in the life made possible by the transformed conceptual understanding.

Learning, on the model of the sublime, occurs in relation to particular instances; occasions that instantiate a new paradigm for consciousness and conceptual understanding. The experiences are idiosyncratic and exemplary: the contingent details of this specific individual or entity at this specific time become the medium by which the necessity of a certain meaning is expressed. It is for this reason that Murdoch represents beauty, with its unique combination of contingency and necessity, as an instance of the sublime. Her classification of beauty as exemplification of the sublime, is also informed by her designation of death as the limit to consciousness – absolute formlessness and nothingness – and her location of it in ordinary mundane and comic life, as well as art, nature and tragedy. Murdoch does not restrict access to the sublime, nor does she elevate a class of individuals (artists, philosophers, children or religious) as having privileged access to it. This is because there is no externally guaranteed science for how to instigate an emergent awareness of the limits of one's consciousness.

Sublimity is not confined to any one activity because all forms of human activity are potentially sublime. In other words, all concepts – 'mud' and 'red' are the examples given by Murdoch – are defined by 'an ideal endpoint' and are 'infinitely to be learned' (*SG*, p. 29). Whether an event or activity induces learning is a matter of what Murdoch refers to as grace: individuals can prepare to deepen their conceptual understanding, they can engage in practices that will make this learning more likely, but they cannot secure it. If learning does happen – if an individual discerns and, in discerning, shifts the limits of his understanding – then it is ultimately a matter of circumstance. Learning is less like something that is the direct result of our efforts and is more like something that we become ready to receive; learning is less a function of freedom and more a function of obedience or, more accurately, given that we are to a certain extent free, it is a function of using our freedom to become more obedient.

For Kant, sublimity distinguished itself by referring us to our nature as reasoners; for Murdoch sublimity distinguishes itself by referring us to and, partially liberating us from, the clutches of psyche or, alternatively, desire. Consciousness is governed by the psyche that is a pernicious, consoling and cunningly self-deceptive, fantasy mechanism – its manoeuvrings are as difficult to identify as they are to circumvent. Sublimity is distinguished by its identification and purification of desire. That this experience is genuine – that the individual's desires are being purified and not just changed – is accepted on faith. This faith is inspired by incrementally cumulative experiences of the sublime and our trust in their verisimilitude. The individual essentially trusts that when she, or another individual, discovers and shifts the particular limitations of her consciousness, she is in effect learning. Individuals approach truth by a process of learning, but the process is infinite; although we approximate to truth we never arrive at it (we never arrive at the sun). If it were possible ever to inhabit truth, then learning would become redundant, and it is learning, not truth, that defines the human condition.

Murdoch represents humility as the most appropriate response to the sublime, as opposed to either Kantian respect (*Achtung*) or romantic irony.[12] This is because Kantian *Achtung* and romantic irony reflect, in her view, the influence of the egoistic fantasy mechanism, celebrating the individual in terms of his moral and creative independence from nature. In both cases, although the individual is subject to nature – death, loss, accident, aging, decay – she is able to transcend nature through free self-creation. Humanity ultimately triumphs and, reigning supreme, vindicates individual striving for freedom. I suggest that Murdoch's conceptualization of the sublime, and its link to humility, can be represented as a feminist intervention in the masculine bias that has historically dominated romantic thinking, particularly if drawing on the literary qualities of her philosophical writing and her use of domestic imagery (mothers; mothers- and daughters-in-law; paying the bills, sweeping the floor, potting plants).

Finally, if Murdoch's philosophy stands as a correction to philosophical heroism, then it also results in a paradox: individuals need to work on the self (curb fantasies, identify fears and evaluate history) if they are to overcome the egoistic limits of their consciousness, and yet, what is increasingly revealed by this more truthful perspective is, precisely, that the self is fundamentally unimportant. Although critically evaluating and disciplining the egoism of the self is absolutely necessary for the possibility of learning – identifying and overcoming the limits of consciousness – the value of this learning resides in its ability to reveal the reality of other people. Murdoch concludes that there is no objective foundation for virtue and that virtue is absolutely necessary. Her underscoring of attention as a just and loving gaze directed to the reality of other individuals is a rejoinder to the romantic focus on *Bildung* as the key to humanity's redemption.[13]

It is the oversights of romanticism that direct Murdoch to designate Plato and Kant (in his more puritan moments) as 'the great romantics'.[14] She endorses the philosophies of these 'great romantics' because they recognize the true limit of consciousness as death and, in so doing, appreciate the simultaneous indefensibility and necessity of responding to other individuals. Working within the broader romantic tradition, Murdoch corrects its most striking anomalies, retrieving a conception of philosophical romanticism exemplified by Plato and, to an extent, Kant. My argument presumes that Murdoch and philosophical romanticism share many background assumptions, including, a common understanding of the limits and possibilities of the philosophical enterprise.

Murdoch and philosophical romanticism

Philosophical romanticism frames my reading of Murdoch, but her philosophy remains in the foreground. The romantic philosophical tradition is complex, inherently diverse and subject to competing interpretations.[15] I present a partial account of philosophical romanticism, informed by my interest in Murdoch's philosophy.[16] Murdoch is not typically associated with the romantic tradition, in part because there has been limited philosophical interest in romanticism – owing to a conception of it as an aesthetic movement dedicated to the revitalization of art – and in part because her arguments address developments in analytic moral philosophy. When Murdoch does refer to romanticism, it is to be critical of its impact on philosophy, literature, art and the cultural imagination.[17] She accuses the romantics of having replaced suffering with death, by taking 'refuge in sublime emotions' (*EM*, p. 368), of making a 'cult of experience' (*SRR*, p. 135) and 'forcing' a 'self-directed enjoyment of nature' (*SG*, p. 85). Her criticisms refer to a romantic strain of thought running through contemporary philosophy, art and culture – an outlook that is idealized, self-inflated and sentimental – that may or may not have its origins in early German romanticism.

I identify the following common reference points for Murdoch and philosophical romanticism. First, Murdoch and the early German romantics are responding to the legacy of Kant's Copernican Revolution. Kant made the subject sovereign over the objective or knowable world – the noumena or thing-in-itself transcends human experience because human experience is necessarily governed by the intuitions and the categories – and prohibits philosophers from ever legitimately theorizing reality from first principles because there exists an attributable subjective derivation. Murdoch cedes to subjectivity its epistemic dominion, accepting that 'human life has no external point or telos' (*SG*, p. 78), and warns philosophers against trying to 'give any single organized background sense to the normative word "reality"' (*SG*, p. 40).

Kant's transcendental idealism makes it theoretically difficult for individuals legitimately to derive meaning or significance from their experience. Reality, as humans can know it, is mechanical, law-governed and inanimate. Kantian and existential philosophies accentuate human independence from the world in the form of human practical reason and genuinely autonomous choice. Post-structuralist theories move in the other direction, emphasizing the complete determination of subjectivity by language. Murdoch shares with philosophical romanticism a reluctance to resolve the Kantian paradox, charting a third or middle ground between absolutism (an objective impersonal unified truth) and subjectivism (proliferating, plural subjective 'truths'). Murdoch and the romantics comprehend, without bridging, the gap between human subjectivity and reality, by bringing the noumenal within the sweep of human experience.

They do not accept that the Kantian 'first principle' entails that reality cannot be discerned or expressed by way of subjective consciousness. Murdoch states that 'we, inside the cave, are intuitively aware of many things whose presence and proximity we may "feel", but which we cannot, or cannot yet, fully explain or inspect' (*MGM*, p. 228). She cites as examples, 'our sense of the presence of a vast extra-linguistic reality ... our sense of history and of unrealized moral possibilities' (*MGM*, p. 228). Like the romantics, Murdoch preserves the Platonic thought that reality is there and we can 'say' a little of what it essentially is.[18] It is more likely to be depicted symbolically: images redescribe a reality that eludes description serving as metaphorical truths. According to Murdoch, 'we study what is higher first "in images"' (*EM*, p. 421). Metaphysical theories do not literally describe reality, but act as barriers or membranes through which reality 'passes'. Murdoch adds that the term reality 'may be used as a philosophical term provided that its limitations are understood' (*SG*, p. 40).

Reality is not readily available to ordinary consciousness, but is 'revealed to the patient eye of love' (*SG*, p. 40). It is discerned through a transformation of ordinary consciousness, and never in its entirety.[19] Murdoch writes that 'we can no longer formulate a general truth about ourselves which shall encompass us like a house. The only satisfied rationalists today are blinkered scientists or Marxists' (*SRR*, p. 113). Reality is 'magnetic but inexhaustible' and our apprehension of it is infinitely perfectible (*SG*, p. 42). Individuals must continually create, dismantle and recreate their conceptual understanding, motivated by longing for wisdom, and a faith that one's perspective is being improved and becoming more truthful.[20] Longing, criticism and self-creation characterize the psychology of the romantics; they are committed, in the language of D.Z. Phillips, 'to a specific picture of human beings as continuous self-interrogators and bearers of aspiration' (Phillips 2002, p. 270).

It is by accepting the possibility of redeeming our understanding, that we express our freedom. This acceptance – freedom as obedience – is reflected in naïvety. Murdoch, in the tradition of philosophical romanticism, privileges naïvety, emphasizing receptivity rather than mastery.[21] This is because the new challenges our sense-making practices, reconfiguring the future and re-evaluating the past.[22] The individual, in an effort to come to terms with the normative authority of the new, revises old concepts and engages new ones; she attempts to think the scarcely thinkable. Murdoch consistently emphasizes new beginnings throughout her literary and philosophical works. In the case of the famous example of M and D, even though D (the daughter-in-law) is dead and M (the mother-in-law) has a 'fixed picture' of D, she is prepared to 'look again' and see anew (*SG*, p. 17). 'Looking again' at D does not cause M to deny her old perspective, but to take account of it. The old picture releases its hold on M's imagination, precisely because the new picture shows it to be 'snobbish', 'prejudiced' and 'narrow-minded' (*SG*, p. 17).

The implication is that M can no longer be as confident in her own judgements, including this new judgement of D. Naïvety exposes us to failure and failure, as Kompridis points out, 'can make us look and feel foolish, pathetic, and unworthy: in risking failure we also risk entering the domain of comedy, where the joke's on us' (2006, p. 50). It emerges that Murdoch, along with philosophical romanticism, conceives of reality as being discovered and created on the model of artistic appreciation and creation. Murdoch and the romantics see art as the uniquely personal expression of what is essentially impersonal, by way of a properly rational imagination. Enlisting Platonic imagery, Murdoch argues that although 'it is *difficult* to look at the sun', we somehow 'retain the idea, and art both expresses and symbolizes it' (*SG*, p. 100). Aestheticization of reality should not set the artist apart from humanity, because 'we all poeticize reality already, and . . . indeed our sense of reality, and of the claims it makes on us, is inseparable from the creative imagination' (Larmore 1996, p. 8).

As stated earlier, Murdoch is not as optimistic as the romantics in her thinking about the extent of an individual's control over the imaginative faculty. Murdoch is acutely aware that although the imagination is the medium by which individuals are reconciled to reality 'in an attitude of natural piety' (Larmore 1996, p. 10), it is also the medium by which individuals flee reality in flights of self-consoling fantasy. In the language of Charles Larmore, 'The visionary power of the imagination can all too naturally expand to the point of seeking to rewrite the world in its own language' (p. 16). Murdoch claims that individuals have only slight control over their imagination, and the control that they do have results from moral discipline. Any attempt to see reality is an exercise in poeticizing the world and becoming morally better. Neither Murdoch nor the romantics accept that surveying the alternative possibilities for action and then choosing between them is tantamount to human freedom and morality. As Margaret Holland explains in her review of *Metaphysics as a Guide to Morals*, 'Murdoch views freedom as a matter of disentangling oneself from illusions in order to see clearly the external world; freedom, according to Murdoch, is clear vision' (1998, p. 180).

Freedom does not involve disentangling oneself from commitments and relationships, but disentangling oneself from illusions about them; it is not radically to sever one's ties with contingency, but to understand truthfully those contingencies – history, family and culture for example – so as to become oneself within the constraints and opportunities that they present. As Murdoch says, 'those who think that freedom is absolute in the "withdraw and reflect" sense confuse the wish with the fact' (*EM*, p. 84). To be free is not to flee from the medium of human existence – from the body, mortality, senseless suffering, accident and misunderstanding – but to seek an expression of meaning that makes the medium of human existence necessary to it; hence the analogy with art.[23] It is the ability to discover necessity and to act meaningfully within it. Differences in freedom constitute moral differences or, alternatively, differences in personal vision or 'configurations of thought' (*EM*, p. 80). 'A morality', Murdoch writes, 'is a ramification of concepts' (*EM*, p. 89).

Both Murdoch and the romantics think of morality as a 'total difference of *Gestalt*' reflected in an individual's 'mode of speech or silence, their choice of words, their assessments of others, their conception of their own lives, what they think attractive or praiseworthy, what they think funny' (*EM*, p. 80–1). It is not that we make different choices in the same world but that 'we see different worlds' (*EM*, p. 80). We do not always understand each others' worlds or concepts and, when such understanding becomes possible it involves the communication 'of completely new, possibly far-reaching and coherent visions' (*EM*, p. 82). Moral change is difficult, 'not easily open to argument', involves 'a considerable area of personal reflection', requires creativity, and may at times fail (*EM*, p. 85). The task of clear vision is endless because it entails emphasizing 'the inexhaustible details of the world', and 'not assuming that one has got individuals and situations "taped"' (*EM*, p. 87).

Murdoch and the romantics define love as realizing our moral commitments within the constraints of our own context. It is the achievement of freedom as obedience. Love is central to both philosophies and defines an enlightened self–world relationship. 'Attention to God', or good, Murdoch writes, 'is a form of love' (*SG*, p. 55). Elsewhere she insists that 'obedience to reality is an exercise of love' (*SG*, p. 42). In other words, love is the mark of the moral agent. Murdoch writes that 'when we try perfectly to love what is imperfect, our love goes out to its object *via* the Good to be thus purified and made unselfish and just' (*SG*, p. 103). Like imagination, love is normally a projection of self: items in the world that an individual encounters have value conditional upon their role in that individual's consciousness: 'False love moves to false good' (*SG*, p. 102). Murdoch defines this love as 'personal', 'invented' and 'subjective', arguing that it is 'too "mechanical" to be a place of vision' (*SG*, p. 75). A purified love is both unconditioned and self-critical (discovering and rediscovering its conditional limitations).

If it is true that love entails that an individual take responsibility for her own consciousness, then it is also true that Murdoch and the romantics cannot be programmatic about how to achieve it. They must, as a result, be open to pluralism. It is an acknowledgement of pluralism, and the provisional status of their claims, that informs the ironical distance evident in Murdoch's and romantic philosophizing. Beiser states that romantic irony begins 'with the constant striving for a system combined with the self-critical awareness that it is unattainable' (Beiser 2003, p. 4). Murdoch theorizes with seriousness as she actively casts doubt upon the objective significance of her claims; she writes authoritatively as she resists being designated as an authority; she defends the reality of the Good and is at the same time reluctant to define, or derive any imperatives for, the good human life. Murdoch insists that we cannot answer the question of what is the highest good for human beings definitively.

Murdoch argues that although human beings cannot define the Good, they experience themselves as oriented towards what they recognize it to be. In other words, the identification of a good individual, act or life is not parasitic upon a theory of the good; rather, 'theories' of the good emerge from events that involve an experience of the good and are educative as to what the good consists in. Philosophical concepts are learned through experience and dialogue. The philosopher–individual creatively takes up a concept, but also awaits communication from others as to the intelligible and exemplary character of her philosophizing.

In the tradition of Murdoch and philosophical romanticism I make, in this book, a personalized use of Murdoch's philosophical concepts, conceiving of it as an exercise in methodological mimesis or iteration. My goal is not to replicate her ideas, but rather to engage in a process of learning them: to see how they bear on my conceptual world. So while it is true that I subsume Murdoch's philosophy under the romantic philosophical tradition – an impersonal, philosophically public and predetermined category – it is also a way of 'going on' with Murdoch's concepts or terms. The romantic philosophical tradition is suitable for such a purpose because it values human subjectivity and objectivity as it is made possible by the individual's conceptual efforts to answer to a reality that she encounters without grasping.

The contribution of such a project is as follows. First, it acknowledges Murdoch's work as being philosophically significant, both in her decision to write philosophy and literature and in the stylistic differences between *The Sovereignty of Good* and *Metaphysics as a Guide to Morals*. Second, it illuminates the philosophical significance of the literary dimensions of Murdoch's philosophical writings – the ironical juxtaposition of imagery, the contrastive play of assertive unequivocal generalization with self-deprecating, doubtful questioning and the coincidence of ordinary language with that of religious and philosophical discourse. Third, it does justice to the philosophical nature of Murdoch's ethics while refraining from a representation of it as 'logical neutral analysis' (*SG*, p. 44). Fourth, it defends Murdoch's philosophy against some of its more recent detractors and criticisms, most notably, that she does not recognize the political and social construction of subjectivity or the value of this recognition for making appropriate moral judgements, and that her construal of moral judgement is too cognitive and objectivist. Fifth, it demonstrates Murdoch's feminism through her linking of romantic aspirations to ordinary consciousness and the domestic sphere.

I conclude this Introduction with a brief outline of the subsequent five chapters. Their order is sequential but not linear. Each chapter is not composed as a discrete step towards a conclusion. Rather the effect is cumulative: chapters are laid over one another, deepening the reader's perspective. The chapters advance the same line of thought across different sites: Murdoch's conception of philosophy, the literary style of her philosophical writings, philosophical romanticism and finally, Murdoch's philosophy.

In Chapter 1, I return to the question of Murdoch's anomalous status within the Anglo-American analytical tradition and represent my interpretation of her philosophy as an acknowledgement, rather than a resolution, of this aspect of her work. I defend my interpretive strategy by grounding it in Murdoch's conception and practice of a philosophy of 'the third way': philosophizing that conceives of philosophical theories as imaginative, artistic unifying forms or pictures that sometimes sparkle with truth. Philosophy, on Murdoch's view, does not have privileged access to reality; it is continuous with and, constrained by, the limits of consciousness: namely final ambiguity. Third-way philosophical theories are religious or mythical in that their so-called 'truth' derives from psychic authority. A central philosophical task, according to Murdoch, is the ongoing evaluation of philosophical theories according to whether their psychic authority derives from either pedagogical efficacy, or what Murdoch terms imaginative capacity – an ability to remind us of what is normally too difficult for us to see, the sheer randomness of human existence and the reality of other individuals – or egoism, what Murdoch terms fantasy – the fulfilment of our desire to think better of ourselves and the world even if by perverse means.

I explain in Chapter 1 how the creation, evaluation, correction and re-creation of philosophical theories requires an imaginative discipline which is also a moral discipline; it also requires an examination of, and experimentation with, different literary and stylistic representations of philosophical thought. It is from Murdoch's conception of philosophy as a third or middle way that I move, in Chapter 2, to a discussion of the literary dimensions of her philosophical writing, including the stylistic development from *The Sovereignty of Good* to *Metaphysics as a Guide to Morals*. I focus on three elements. First, there is her at times playful and at times sinister reference to temperament as a constant source of philosophical motivation. She identifies temperament as the potential source of both her critiques and arguments. Second, I highlight the myriad ways in which Murdoch enlists irony in her philosophical writings: she uses irony to signal the incompleteness of her own philosophical theorizing; to challenge the presumption of philosophical and religious privilege; and to destabilize condescension towards ordinary consciousness. Third, I focus on the dialogical character of Murdoch's philosophy and philosophical development: she does not use philosophical terminology; she revises her philosophical writing and thinking in light of others' responses to it; she adopts, in *Metaphysics as Guide to Morals*, a more relaxed, conversational and muddled philosophical literary style.

In the latter half of Chapter 2 I represent Murdoch's elucidation of two philosophies of 'the third way', namely Plato's and Kant's. Murdoch terms their respective philosophies 'religious' because, in her view, Plato and Kant are cognizant of the mythical status of their theories and concerned that their theories have an educative rather than a merely descriptive effect. Their intention, despite appearances, is not to describe reality so much as it is to describe the character of our relationship to reality in an effort to correct erroneous engagements with it. They understand that a satisfactory philosophy, whether it is aesthetics, ethics, or psychology, must give a rich account of what we unphilosophically know to be the case. I elucidate Murdoch's interpretation of these philosophies, illustrating some of her more central claims.

Chapter 3 provides a context for Chapters 4 and 5, by describing the central characteristics of romantic thought. The chapter reiterates many of the features enumerated above, but with exclusive reference to romanticism. It relies on Frederick Beiser's (2003) analysis of early German romanticism, focusing on Friedric Schelling, Kare Schlegel and Novalis, for two reasons. First, Beiser represents romanticism as an ethical movement and, second, his analysis of it as an ethical movement is made possible by his focus on his subjects' Platonism. In other words, Beiser's conception of romanticism as the 'greatest revival of Platonism since the Renaissance' (Beiser 2003, p. 59) facilitates his determination of it as an ethical movement, and vice versa. It is in the context of Beiser's analysis that I highlight the following features: romanticism's historical foundations in Kant, the revival of Plato, the concepts of love and *Bildung*, and the role of literary form, irony and self-criticism in their thought.

In Chapter 4 I argue that Murdoch's relationship to philosophical romanticism is much more ambivalent than her criticisms suggest. Drawing on Platonic mythology, Murdoch represents the romantics as looking at the fire – the self and its suffering freedom – as opposed to the sun – meaninglessness and the resulting reality of others. The romantics are only half-way to becoming enlightened, because they fail to acknowledge our 'fallen' human condition as reflected in their optimistic and elitist theory of human personality: self-realization, conceived of as a process of independent, isolated and creative self-expression as the ultimate human achievement. Murdoch juxtaposes this heroic conception and evaluation of self-realization with instances of unheroic, humble, loving service to others: the work of mothers, social workers, teachers and civil servants, for example. She argues that correcting the masculine bias of romantic thought – disciplining its desire for the self's triumphant overcoming of suffering – will reorient philosophical romanticism towards an appreciation for the true reality of chance and a desire to know and coexist with other human beings. It is in the context of this argument that I explain Murdoch's distinction between romanticism and 'the great Romantics' and her vulnerability to contemporary criticisms of philosophical romanticism.

In Chapter 5 I outline my interpretation of Murdoch's philosophy, focusing on her conception of the sublime as a corrective to Kantian and romantic conceptions. Murdoch writes in this regard that 'what stuns us into a realization of our supersensible destiny is not, as Kant imagined, the formlessness of nature, but rather its unutterable particularity; and most particular and individual of all natural things is the mind of man' (*EM*, p. 215). To realize our supersensible destiny is not to feel awe or respect, as secured by our identity of reasoners; rather it is to feel humility, inspired by the infinite perfectibility of coming to truth and goodness, and love for particularity and contingency. Murdoch's central insight is to designate the sublime as pedagogical, not on the basis of its ability to disclose our a priori reason – Kant's fundamental mistake – but on the basis of its ability to reveal the limits of our form-giving, imaginatively unifying consciousness, by pointing to more truthful possibilities. Murdoch's commitment to pedagogical necessity of the sublime can be formulated in two ways: as the differentiation of egoistical consciousness in the intimation of less egoistical possibilities; and as the differentiation of a love that is base and self-serving in a dignifying reorientation of it. I demonstrate how the meaning of these and other Murdochian terms such as, 'good' and 'attention' for example, can be understood in relation to philosophical romanticism.

I use literary examples throughout the book to elucidate and amplify Murdoch's central concepts.[24] These literary examples include: J.M. Coetzee's *Elizabeth Costello*, Peter Pouncey's *Rules for Old Men Waiting* and E. Annie Proulx's *The Shipping News*. I consciously choose literature other than Murdoch's own novels in order to demonstrate that her philosophy provides a framework for reading all, not just her own, fiction. I recognize that the relationship between philosophy and literature is ambiguous and deserves far greater analysis, particularly in light of recent scholarly developments (Stanley Cavell, Jacques Derrida, Michelle Le Doeuff, Genevieve Lloyd, Paul Ricoeur and Richard Rorty), Murdoch's philosophical reflections on art and her dual status as novelist and philosopher. At the risk of inviting accusations of naïvety, I side-step these debates, using fictionalized intrapersonal and interpersonal events from these novels in the service of my exposition. Although I do not comment on the literary or philosophical status of these novels, my use of them is not merely instrumental, for they are used alongside Murdoch's philosophy to amplify and develop her thought.

Although I do not argue for it here, my view is that Murdoch would approve of my approach to these literary examples. My use of them does not imply that philosophy and literature are fundamentally different but represents them as, quoting Lloyd, 'different kinds of "fiction" through which we may come to a deeper understanding' of human experience.[25] Although philosophy utilizes concepts and literature utilizes characters, both involve the operation of images, inviting an emotional response and pointing us in the direction of truth.

Chapter 1

A Philosophy of the 'Third Way'[1]

Introduction

Conscious of an inescapable tension inherent in our reading of philosophical texts, Murdoch writes that

> In thinking about the world of great metaphysicians one has to seek a balance between 'faithfulness to the text' and a tendency to invent one's own metaphysician. If one is too 'faithful', one may merely reproduce unassimilated ideas which remain remote and dead; if one is too 'inventive', one may lose the original and present one's own thoughts instead of the great thought to which one should have attended more carefully. (*MGM*, p. 510)

Murdoch argues against reading texts too faithfully, because this results in the mere reproduction of ideas which remain unassimilated and so 'remote and dead'. Reading a text does not involve identifying rules it enlists to dictate the use of its terms – this is to be too 'faithful'. Rather, the hermeneutical task is to assimilate the ideas so that they transform our thinking. It is to make 'a personalized *use*' of them (*SG*, p. 2). A personalized use of concepts, as distinct from either 'faithfulness' or 'inventiveness', engages 'the whole mind' of the reader, which is to say that it bears on the conceptual world of the reader (Diamond 1988, p. 273).[2]

The significant challenge, then, is to prevent the ideas of the text being lost, as they are translated, by and into, the conceptual world of the reader. Murdoch argues against reading too inventively because this amounts to presenting our own thoughts in the guise of another's. She admits her concern over 'the danger of inventing [her] own Plato and extracting a particular pattern from his many-patterned text to reassure [herself] that, as [she sees] it, good is really good and real is really real' (*MGM*, p. 510). Murdoch advocates that philosophers 'attempt to write in ordinary language and not in jargon' in order to ensure that readers correctly understand the ideas presented (*MGM*, p. 172). Philosophy's task is to help 'preserve and refresh a stream of meticulous, subtle, eloquent ordinary language, free from jargon and able to deal clearly and in detail with matters of a certain degree of generality and abstraction' (*MGM*, p. 211).

The eloquent use of ordinary language is part of what Murdoch refers to as philosophy's 'return ... towards the consideration of simple and obvious facts' (*SG*, p. 1). An instance of such a return is when Moore responds to McTaggart's claim that time is unreal by saying that 'he has just had breakfast' (*SG*, p. 1). This 'movement of return' is more than just semantic because it retrieves the facts 'theorized away' by 'the elaborate theories' (*SG*, p. 1). It is a way of calling us back to ourselves. It reflects an abiding philosophical concern for ordinary consciousness and everyday life: our daily routines and everyday practices (playing with our children, ringing our parents, making lunches and enjoying a glass of wine with dinner, for example); the many secular and religious rituals (marriage ceremonies, funerals and birthday celebrations); our fears, fantasies, joys, hopes and frustrations; as well as contingency, sexuality, personal histories and relationships.[3] Through this 'movement of return' philosophy becomes 'inhabited', infusing the minds of individuals and becoming a philosophy that they can live by (*SG*, p. 47). Philosophy conceived of in this way speaks to our sense of ourselves and our lives; it works with what is already there conceptually and phenomenologically. According to Murdoch, 'Philosophy puts things in places and surrounds them with many considerations. The image of the field of force is good here' (*MGM*, p. 378).[4]

I wish to engage in just such a return, calling to mind and coming to terms with Murdoch's distinctiveness as a philosopher. My reading strategy results from a participation with Murdoch's texts that entails 'following out its gestures of sense-making from the inside' (Eldridge 2001, p. 69). I consider her commitment to what she, as an individual, feels compelled to say by considering her examples and images; a personal and often idiosyncratic appropriation of the Western tradition; the conscious stylistic changes between her earlier and later philosophical writings;[5] her acknowledgement of the power of the human psyche to distort or reveal 'reality'; the interplay, in her works, between her public and private speech, aspiration and disappointment, confident lucidity and doubts; and, ultimately, her use of irony.

The chapter is divided into two sections. I begin with a discussion of Murdoch's version of Kant's Copernican Revolution and her representation of human consciousness. I draw on the writings of Garrett Green and Ann Denham to elucidate Murdoch's theory of consciousness as imaginative, perceptual and, potentially, 'objective'. I begin with her theory of consciousness because it is foundational for her view of philosophy. Philosophy is, after all, a product of human consciousness and, as a product of

A Philosophy of the Third Way　　19

human consciousness, is perspectival, pictorial and partial. It is developed and spoken by an 'I'. This 'I' is not solipsistic, but exists in dialogical relationship with a reality that exceeds comprehension and is continually being brought within its horizons. This reality includes other individuals that are, as an 'I', experienced as a 'you'.

The second section of the chapter addresses Murdoch's conception of philosophy because it is informed by her understanding of consciousness. She argues for a philosophy of the 'third way' – a phrase taken from her first philosophical book, *Sartre: Romantic Rationalist*. In her discussions of Plato and Kant as philosophers of the 'third way', Murdoch refers to their philosophies as 'religious'. I find the term 'third way' preferable for the reasons that it is more descriptive and less associative (see Chapter 2). A philosophy of the 'third way' acknowledges its status as a *broken totality*, informed by the recognition that philosophizing, like ordinary consciousness, imagines reality (as a totality). In other words, a philosophical outlook does not describe reality directly; rather it alludes to what reality is like by way of how it depicts it. Anchored in the psyche, philosophizing is equally susceptible to the egoistic fantasy mechanism and the overwhelming desire for comfort, consolation and aggrandizement. Philosophers must be morally vigilant in guarding against the effects of their individual psyches; philosophical truth-seeking is no different from the truth-seeking of ordinary consciousness.

Murdoch on human consciousness and imagination

Murdoch's conception of philosophy of the third or middle way originates in her characterization of ordinary human consciousness as 'a deep continuous working of values, a *continuous present and presence* of perceptions, intuitions, images, feelings, desires, aversions, attachments' (*MGM*, p. 215). Here she is not referring to the values which an individual self-consciously adheres but to those values that consciously or unconsciously influence an individual's conceptualizations. We are 'pattern-makers' (*SG*, p. 65), 'constantly conceptualizing what confronts us, "making" it into meaning, into language' (*MGM*, p. 195). Conceptualizations inform what we ' "see things as", what we let, or make ourselves think about' (*MGM*, p. 215). Values frame our experience of reality. Murdoch writes that 'at deep levels metaphor and perception merge. Perception is a mode of evaluation' (*MGM*, p. 328).

Consciousness only ever frames or informs our experience of reality because 'what we encounter remains free, ambiguous, endlessly contingent, and *there*' (*MGM*, p. 195). There is something there for consciousness to meet, even though the meeting is always mediated by consciousness and the necessity of seeing it as one thing rather than another. Consciousness is the expression of values, and values are expressed by how they allow us to imagine and see reality or the 'order and pattern' that they indicate (*MGM*, p. 327). It follows that imagination and metaphor not only play a role in aesthetics, they also shape 'our private unclarified but often strong and present thinking and experience' (*MGM*, p. 328).

In order to understand ordinary consciousness it is instructive to look at artistic creativity. Although the '"breeding of imagery" is a familiar aspect of our moment-to-moment, minute-to-minute, hour-to-hour "consciousness"', it goes on without our conscious awareness (*MGM*, p. 330). How consciousness is operating is submerged in *the* operation of consciousness. Murdoch writes that 'so deep is imagery in life that one may not always realize or know whether one is regarding something as itself, or as an image' (*MGM*, p. 505). We find that there are rare moments when an individual can become aware of his consciousness from the perspective of the observer. This awareness is inspired by such occasions as attending to something new, attending to a familiar object or person in a new way, learning a language, or becoming absorbed in artistic or creative endeavour. On these occasions individuals 'experience the force and movement of imagination' and are compelled to revisit former consciousness, discarding old imagery in seeking new, and improved, images (*MGM*, p. 322).

In his analysis of Murdoch's fiction, Peter Conradi aptly describes this process as iconoclastic, referring less to the substance of these images and more to their epistemic and psychological force. Imbued with immense power and significance, icons inspire reverence, prayer, motivation, resilience, resistance and, on occasion, martyrdom. Icons come to be discarded when their persuasive force is no longer felt. At the point of being no longer necessary, the icon becomes just like any other invented image: the production of a mere individual. The invented image remains intelligible but is no longer meaningful in the way that it was when it operated as a an icon. Consciousness is iconoclastic in that it operates 'by developing imagery and also by discarding it' (*MGM*, p. 327). Imagery enables individuals to behave in the world in the way that they do: it is the image of the 'family' that inspires parents to make significant personal sacrifices for their children (be a stay-at-home parent, work two jobs, move school districts, have child-friendly holidays); it is the image of the 'hero' that motivates individuals to join the services (police, fire, ambulance, military) and risk their lives each day.

Changing our images, changes what is possible for us in terms of our life choices. This is why 'an important part of human learning is an ability both to generate and to judge and understand the imagery which helps us to interpret the world' (*MGM*, p. 215). It is an important part of human learning for reasons not only to do with action, but also truth, as some images are more truthful than others. The development of ordinary consciousness in the direction of greater truthfulness is a progress away from the falsifying 'egoistic fantasies' at one end towards the 'creative imagination, culminating in genius at the other' (*MGM*, p. 320). Murdoch's 'distinction between "*fantasy*" as mechanistic, egoistic, untruthful, and "*imagination*" as truthful and free' relies upon a difference in the orientation and source of our imagination (*MGM*, p. 321).

Murdoch enlists art as the best model for consciousness, because whereas most (bad) art illustrates our inability to resist our self-consoling and self-aggrandizing fantasy mechanism, truly great art resists such temptation and 'shows us the world, our world and not another one, with a clarity which startles and delights us simply because we are not used to looking at the real world at all' (*SG*, p. 65). How do we know the difference between fantasy-ridden and great impersonal art? Murdoch's answer is simple. People believe they know the difference, and 'it takes quite a lot of theorizing to persuade them to say or imagine that they do not' (*MGM*, p. 496). The reason that people believe they can know the difference between bad and good art is love (other words that might be used to convey the same idea are reverence, awe, respect and admiration). Individuals judge as 'good' those art works that they love, and they love art works that they think of as 'showing [them] the world'. It is very difficult for individuals to love what they conceive of as debased, petty, ugly or self-serving, for example. The exception is human pathology. Pathology is the inversion of health, so rather than esteeming what is lovable, the individual esteems what is base; rather than seeking love the individual considers himself unworthy of love. In either case, love metamorphoses into 'ambition, vanity, cruelty, jealousy, hatred, or the parched demoralizing deserts of its absence' (*MGM*, p. 497).

Of course individuals can be mistaken about what is worthy of love. An individual might, for example, cherish a bad piece of art under the mis conception of it as good. Murdoch equivocates on this point: sometimes she appears to be arguing that anything is a potential object of love – if mud can be, then why not concentration camp guards, pornography, serial killers, mass murderers and dictators? – and at other times she appears to defend a love that is far more discerning. She wants to leave open the possibility that both are true. On one hand, the incompleteness of human learning entails that individuals must remain open to 'inconceivable' possibilities: for example, that an unrepentant, vile and egregious criminal might be the intelligible object of love. On the other hand, she recognizes that in loving certain images and not others, consciousness inevitably casts its judgement, precluding the intelligibility of some possibilities and not others. In my view, this paradox is definitive of Murdoch's approach to morality and moral philosophy. She insists that individuals must take responsibility for the responsiveness of their consciousness in the recognition that individuals do this from a position of partial ignorance; humanity is encumbered by the requirements to live and to reconsider one's life (opening up the possibility for new ways of living).

It is no accident, in Murdoch's view, that individuals (even right up until their death) ask themselves whether they did the right thing by having or not having children; whether they could have been kinder to their spouse; whether they made the most out of their opportunities; whether they should have looked after their parents or whether they could have forgiven an earlier betrayal. These questions are asked, in part, because there is no 'objective' standpoint from which to see the whole and so provide a definitive answer to them – the questions are asked by mere individuals existing in relationship with other mere individuals. These questions are also asked, in part, because individuals seek not just any answer, but the right answer; we want to be reassured that we did not love ourselves and others poorly. It is human finitude combined with a deep desire on the part of humanity to be moral, and therefore right, that drives this relentless questioning.

An illustration of how it is that human beings strive for moral determinacy, in its absence, is to be found in J.M. Coetzee's recent novel, *Elizabeth Costello* (henceforth referred to as *EC*).[6] The incident concerns the main character, Elizabeth, a 60-year-old, moderately successful Australian author. Elizabeth is divorced with two adult children, gives public lectures and is preoccupied by the treatment of animals. Her only sister, Blanche, otherwise known as Sister Bridget of the Sisters of Marian Order, administers a hospital in Zululand, South Africa, for which she is awarded an honorary doctorate. Elizabeth attends the award ceremony and discovers that Blanche conceives of herself as being in fundamental disagreement with Elizabeth, having chosen Christianity over Elizabeth's humanism. Blanche accuses Elizabeth of having backed 'a loser' by going 'for the wrong Greeks' (*EC*, p. 145). She explains to Elizabeth that 'ordinary people do not want the Greeks. They do not want the realm of pure forms. They do not want marble statues. They want someone who suffers like them. Like them and for them' (*EC*, p. 144). Elizabeth notices not the suffering, but the unrelenting and overwhelming preoccupation with suffering, represented by the abundant crucifixion iconography.

It is in the context of this 'dispute', that Elizabeth recalls an event involving her then elderly, mother's 'friend', Mr Phillips, an artist dying from

A Philosophy of the Third Way

the ravages of age, cancer and cancer treatment. At her mother's bequest, Elizabeth sits for Mr Phillips. No longer able to speak, he writes to her on a notepad that there was a time when he would have painted her nude, at which point she removes her top. Describing the moment to Blanche in a letter, she writes:

> Whether it worked, whether the spectacle of me in the seminude rekindled anything in him, I cannot say. But I could feel the full weight of his gaze on me, on my breast, and frankly, it was good. I was forty then, I had two children behind me, they were not the breasts of a young woman, but it was nevertheless, I thought so and think so still, in that place of withering away and dying a blessing. (*EC*, p. 148)

Elizabeth remains puzzled by her own motivation for, as she describes, 'gazing calmly into the distance with my robe hanging about my waist like a cloud and my divine body on show' (*EC*, p. 149). She admits of both classical and Christian associations: Greek because, as she says of herself, 'through me a goddess was manifesting herself, Aphrodite or Hera or perhaps even Artemis. I was of the immortals'; Christian because like the Virgin Mary, Elizabeth tips 'her sweet pink nipple up' for Mr Phillips, succoring him as Mary succoured Jesus.

Christianity and humanism give Elizabeth ways to understand her motivation, but it does not resolve the issue of whether what she did was right – that choice will not be resolved theoretically. This idea is taken further when the reader learns that on a future visit Elizabeth gives Mr Phillips unprompted fellatio (this fact is not shared with Blanche). Elizabeth considers her second gesture to be as noble as the first – she *wants* to be able to acknowledge it as an act of love in the ethical and not erotic sense – but given the unavailability of cultural precedents, she wonders if she is right to think so. She might after all be self-deceived, but she recognizes that the answer does not lie in the rightness or wrongness of humanism or Christianity, for as she explains:

> In all our talk about humanism and the humanities there was a word we both skirted: *humanity*. When Mary blessed among women smiles her remote angelic smile and tips her sweet pink nipple up before our gaze, when I, imitating her, uncover my breasts for old Mr Phillips, we perform acts of humanity. Acts like that are not available to animals, who cannot uncover themselves because they do not cover themselves. Nothing compels us to do it, Mary or me. But out of the overflow, the outflow of our

human hearts, we do it nevertheless; drop our robes, reveal ourselves, reveal the life and beauty we are blessed with. (*EC*, p. 148)

Elizabeth wants to be able to speak about her act as love or *caritas* because she feels that she was responding to the isolation and pain of Mr Phillips' suffering by sharing with him a moment of beauty, and even joy, perhaps. The particularities of the situation take on a universal quality for Elizabeth and potentially the reader, because together they exemplify our human vulnerability and reciprocity – Elizabeth's gesture gives life to an idea that defines us in our humanity. Yet she continues to ruminate on the experience because she senses that other individuals – including her own self at a later time – might not be persuaded to see and understand it in the same way; the situation could so easily slip into appearing otherwise. She asks herself, 'What can one make of episodes like this, unforeseen, unplanned, out of character? Are they just holes, holes in the heart, into which one steps and falls and then goes on falling?' (*EC*, p. 155). The 'holes', holes in which we all enter, exemplify the combined clarity and ambiguity of consciousness, mentioned earlier. Their idiosyncratic newness entails that they have not yet been reduced to a set of organized beliefs, and yet call out for just such organization and understanding, for it is only through such articulation and re-articulation of understanding, that individuals are able to appreciate the limitations of that understanding, inviting further transcendence and the creation of new 'holes'. Understanding is important for us not because it conclusively pins down reality, but because it joins us to reality, making possibilities for new ways of relating possible.

The example of *Elizabeth Costello* is included here to illustrate that Murdoch intends by her philosophy and fiction to avoid the opposition between truth conceived as either wholly annexed to an independent reality that consciousness is required to accurately replicate – an alternative metaphorically represented by the mirror – or as wholly annexed to a productive human subjectivity which proliferates freely chosen and created 'realities' – another alternative metaphorically represented by the lamp (Mulhall 1997, p. 233). Each alternative presents its own problem or limit. In the case of the mirror, consciousness is threatened by an inability accurately to reproduce reality (distortion) and get outside itself in order to determine its own accuracy (scepticism). In the case of the lamp, consciousness is threatened by its own arbitrariness and the question of which 'reality' to trust. Murdoch insists that accepting either of the above alternatives deprives human life of its ultimate indeterminacy and infinite capacity for learning.

Murdoch introduces a third, mediating, alternative that conceives of reality and the individual as equally necessary elements of truth, in the paradox of our humanness. Truth and falsehood are 'created' in the 'meeting' of a unifying and form-giving consciousness with a formless and incomplete reality. Although human consciousness forms 'reality', it does not determine it. Murdoch repeatedly stresses that if either the subject's creativity or truth-seeking are left out at the beginning, then it becomes impossible to put them in later (*MGM*, p. 243).

Garrett Green's metaphor of the *lens* accurately represents Murdoch's third alternative. A lens is something that we see with rather than look at. We become aware of a lens through its absence rather than its presence. A lens is a focusing device that facilitates the identification of what might otherwise be missed. When the imagination serves as a lens in this way, it has a clarifying and interpretive function that, in Green's words, 'allows us to see something as meaningful – that is, filled with meaning, having significance rather than sheer randomness' (Green 2002, p. 78). A lens not only focuses reality: it can project images and narratives that may or may not be realistic. In this case the imagination creates fictions, fantasies, stories and archetypes that may or may not have a bearing on reality. Acting in this capacity, it presents models for human behaviour and understanding through images and stories that provoke, inspire and instruct. Murdoch cites examples from the New Testament – the story of the woman who broke the alabaster box of precious ointment, and the parable of the prodigal son – as fictions that incarnate concrete and paradoxical moral truths, 'open to continual reinterpretation' (*EM*, p. 91).

Through the metaphor of the lens, Green characterizes the imagination as paradigmatic and exemplary. It is paradigmatic because it recognizes 'the constitutive pattern that makes a thing what it is and not something else'; it is exemplary because 'it is the ability to see one thing *as* another, to recognize in a familiar and accessible image the heuristic model that illuminates another, more complex or recalcitrant aspect of the world' (Green 2002, pp. 81–2). Green's representation of the analogical faculty of the imagination accords with Murdoch's. Figurative language 'is everywhere in our thinking', changing with changes to an individual's interests, relationships and experiences. And yet inherent in the constancy of change is the sense that there is 'something "deeper" or "beyond"', which the imagery evokes or points to' (*MGM*, p. 171). Metaphor is apprehended by the thinker 'as ultimate or as pointing beyond' (*MGM*, p. 171).

For Green, the metaphor of the lens usefully 'combines features of both the "reproductive" aspect of the mirror (imagination as mimetic) and the "productive" aspect of the lamp (imagination as creative)' (Green 2002, p. 78). Murdoch's metaphor of vision also combines the reproductive and productive aspects of the imagination, as well as showing the interrelationship between the two. As with the lens, vision has multiple references. It refers to our ability to see what is simply and obviously there, as in the case of seeing our toes or a striped shirt – this is its reproductive aspect. It 'gathers up and focuses the data we intuit into coherent patterns' (Green 2002, p. 81). Vision also refers to our ability to see what is not so obviously there. For example, the case of Cassandra's prophetic revelations or Buddha's mystical insights illustrate the reproductive aspect with an emphasis on its framing dimension. Vision also refers to the ideals by which we live and against which we determine our life. This is the productive aspect of the imagination, but the reproductive is never far away. For it is against the background of such visions that we interpret experience and, in the language of Green, 'turn marks on a page, or sounds in the ear, into meaning-filled language' (2002, p. 78).

Denham (2001) helps build and extend the argument. Admittedly, she does not use terms such as 'consciousness' and 'imagination', choosing instead to restrict her analysis to Murdoch's meta-ethics (the epistemic status of moral judgements) and moral psychology (describing the nature of moral experience), but her conclusions remain relevant. This is because a critical part of Murdoch's argument is the thesis that *all* human experience – and not just the evidently moral kind – is characterized by its ethical dimensions (Denham 2001, pp. 602–29).[7] In her article, Denham introduces a term of art – aspectual properties – to explain Murdoch's characterization of concepts, particularly moral ones, as inherently configurational, that is, as 'marking out evaluative facts' (p. 614). These evaluative facts are, she argues, kinds of aspectual properties analogous to both pictorial and musical aspects.

Denham builds the analogy between evaluative and these other aspects, by distinguishing between two types of properties: 'base' or 'subvenient' properties (she gives the example of lines and colours on a canvas; and the sequence of sounded tones) and 'supervenient' properties (the pictorial aspects of a painting like 'tree-depiction or a flower-depiction or a face-depiction'; and 'musical aspects such as the melodic, the rhythmic, the dissonant, the harmonious') (Denham 2001, p. 611). She argues that individuals experience the supervenient properties directly in experience; they are perceptual judgements and so not inferred from the base properties on which they depend. An individual's experience of a portrait or melody is non-inferential. Denham concludes that

> when we say that someone is able to discern pictorial aspects – that he possesses 'pictorial competence' – we are not imputing to him any special visual faculty; we just impute to him a wholly ordinary capacity for

A Philosophy of the Third Way 27

pictorial seeing-as – for discerning the pictorial aspects by looking at the properties on which they supervene. (p. 610)

She argues that it is similarly the case with 'hearing-as.'

'Seeing-as' and 'hearing-as' are ordinary capacities for, as Denham describes, discerning the aspectual properties of sights and sounds. She suggests that something analogous (although not parallel) occurs in the case of moral judgements. She argues that moral judgement, 'like basic pictorial and musical judgments, arise from our experience of configured aspects of value' (Murdoch's 'deep configurations of the world'), and occur by way of our responsiveness to the subvenient features on which those aspects depend (Denham 2001, p. 613). Denham identifies the 'best and most obvious candidates' for these subvenient properties 'as persons' concerns and interests – the wants, needs, and purposes of other subjects of experience, others who, like oneself, inhabit a world of values' (p. 613).

Denham's analogy between evaluative and other kinds of aspects produces similar insights to Green's image of the lens. She argues that moral aspects supervene on non-moral properties, but are not – and this is important – entirely reducible to them. Denham states that

> Likewise, what it is to be say, cowardly, or unkind or courageous or just cannot be fully analyzed in terms of some other, nonmoral properties. But this is not because they fail to be genuine 'facts' on par with natural ones. Rather, it is because they are, qua aspectual facts, only directly evident to those who possess the requisite experiential sensitivity. Hence the analogy also suggests that moral aspects are perspectival: whether one detects them depends on one's experiential capacities and point of view. (Denham 2001, p. 614)

In the language of the previous discussion, concepts respond to reality but do not straightforwardly 'reproduce' it by virtue of the fact that they also organize it. As Denham points out, conceptual patterns are not all qualitatively the same – we are not reduced to accepting a bland form of relativism – for some turn out to be more illuminative, (i.e. truthful) than others. They require a greater degree of 'experiential sensitivity', which takes time and learning, being it is the result of practice, dedication, discipline, self-reflection and self-correction.

Other images that Murdoch uses to highlight the productive and reproductive features of the imagination include the barrier, band or lungs. The point of these images is to highlight how consciousness is both inescapably creative and penetrable. Although consciousness marks out the limits of reality, containing and controlling, it is porous like a sponge, enabling elements of reality to pass into it (*MGM*, p. 315). The problem is one of detection – determining what is reality and what is consciousness – because reality is transformed as it enters consciousness. These images acknowledge what Green refers to as the 'undecidability' of the imagination and the 'inevitability of interpretation.' The imagination is 'undecidable' because it simultaneously reproduces into an 'an organized gestalt whatever aspect of reality we are apprehending' and 'performs a "creative" task, forming the raw material of intuition into meaningful shapes and sounds that we can recognize' (Green 2002, pp. 81–2). What is the case remains ambiguous. All that can be hoped for is interpretation. There is no accessible independent ground upon which all interpretation rests. We cannot, in Murdoch's terms, 'descend by any unitary "scientific" or systematic method below the levels at which, in various ways, we test truth and reflect upon moral understanding' (*MGM*, p. 242). Interpretation, therefore, involves the ongoing identification, criticism and revision of the subjective paradigms that necessarily frame experience as we look for those interpretations that service *'truth-telling.'*[8]

Ambiguity is the fundamental limit, making it impossible to know with certainty whether an interpretive framework is truly conveying reality or simply shielding us from it. Murdoch says that 'at every level of sophistication we have to beware, on our way, of idolatry and false deities' (*MGM*, p. 496). Although our relationship to truth is ultimately ambiguous, it is not a reason to despair. This is because it seems, wherever we look, that it is possible for human beings to 'make their way', to witness progress and become transformed. Murdoch writes that

> On the road between illusion and reality there are many clues and signals and wayside shrines and sacraments and places of meditation and refreshment. The pilgrim just has to look about him with a lively eye. There are many kinds of images in the world, sources of energy, checks and reminders, pure things, inspiring things, innocent things, attracting love and veneration. We all have our own icons, untainted and vital, which we, perhaps secretly, store away in safety. There is nothing esoteric or surprising about this, people know it, it is familiar. (*MGM*, pp. 496)

Interestingly, but not surprisingly, these checks and reminders serve to remind us of ourselves as given in relation to reality, rather than as being indicators of reality itself. They remind us of the difference between a purified love and an abject one. As in the case of an artist's muse or a lover's beloved, these images and icons serve as a source of positive energy and the positive energy is in turn used to verify the worthiness of the muse or beloved. Murdoch admits there is an inescapable circularity here, but does not accept it as vicious.

Murdoch's position is rooted in 'instances of the facts' (*SG*, p. 1). For example, individuals are claimed by what they 'see' or appreciate, and vision or appreciation is grounded in conceptual understanding; conceptual understanding is not static but evolves historically; art and experience are instrumental in 'altering and complicating' an individual's conceptual evolution (*SG*, p. 29); individuals measure progress in relation to self, concepts and relationships. Murdoch refers to these tenets when she states that she is offering 'a kind of inconclusive non-dogmatic naturalism' (*SG*, p. 44). The content of her naturalism is human learning. If human beings knew 'the truth', then living as we know it would cease to exist, but likewise, if human beings were to abandon the search for 'the truth', then we would no longer have an impetus for life as we know it.

Murdoch's characterization of human consciousness has implications for the practice and epistemic status of the discipline of philosophy.

Murdoch's philosophy of the third way

For Murdoch, philosophy, like art, exemplifies rather than transcends consciousness; it is a form of imaginative framing.[9] Human beings think about abstract matters and, in thinking about abstract matters, 'instinctively produce images' (*MGM*, p. 35). She writes that 'Metaphysics is full of metaphors whose force is often half concealed' (*MGM*, p. 177). She rejects the conception that imagery is the exclusive preserve of myth and religion, arguing that 'if the demythologization of theological and moral thinking means the removal of picture, can this be more than a substitution of one picture for another, so that (for instance) instead of God we have the mobile jumping will, and instead of metaphors of light, metaphors of movement' (*MGM*, pp. 36–7).

As with the image of the lens and vision, philosophy combines the productive and reproductive elements of the imagination. In *The Sovereignty of Good* Murdoch characterizes philosophy as a two-way 'movement towards the building of elaborate theories, and ... back again towards the consideration of simple and obvious facts' (*SG*, p. 1). In *Metaphysics as a Guide to Morals*, she characterizes it in terms of a 'tension between empiricism and metaphysics, between, one might say, Moore and McTaggart' (*MGM*, p. 211). It can, Murdoch says, 'take place within the same philosopher' who engages in an ongoing movement 'between simplicity and elaboration' (*MGM*, p. 211).

She recognizes that 'there are times for piecemeal analysis, modesty and common sense, and other times for ambitious synthesis and the aspiring and edifying charm of lofty and intricate structures' (*MGM*, p. 211). Whereas ordinary consciousness is engaged with this or that aspect of life or the world, philosophy is engaged with the question of life as a whole, reality in its entirety or 'the world *as such*' (Green 2002, p. 84). It seeks to understand what 'the all' is like; for a way to picture or conceptualize the ultimate foundations or the 'ultimate frame of reference' (Green 2002, p. 84).

Murdoch writes that 'philosophers hanker after deep foundations and describable (even if postulated) entities' (*MGM*, p. 259). 'The image of a unified limited whole is a product of philosophical art, and is like a work of art' (*MGM*, p. 35). For the desire to speak of 'everything that is' as a 'whole' or unity 'works deeply' in religion, physics, philosophy and ordinary consciousness. This aspiration is not a naïvely ambitious extension of reason because 'objects', 'things' and 'people' are 'whole-making' unities of a smaller scale. It is an impulse that extends from physics to ordinary consciousness, for to think *is* to think in 'unified limited wholes', no matter how apparently artificial. A particular metaphysical theory may turn out to be an illusion, but thinking metaphysically is 'natural and inevitable'.

If philosophy is continuous with ordinary consciousness, then its limits are the limits of ordinary consciousness, namely ambiguity. Murdoch writes that 'what is "deep" in philosophy is not something literal or quasi-factual or quasi-scientific' but rather something metaphorical (*MGM*, p. 236). Philosophy depicts reality in terms of our relationship to it. 'Formal philosophy can come only so far, and after that can only point' (*MGM*, p. 236). She elucidates:

> From here we may see that the task of moral philosophers has been to extend, as poets may extend, the limits of the language, and enable it to illuminate regions of reality which were formally dark. Where the attempt fails, and one has to choose without having understood, the virtues of faith and hope have their place. It is very well to say that one should always attempt a full understanding and a precise description, but to say that one can always be confident that one has understood seems plainly unrealistic. There are even moments when understanding *ought* to be withheld. (*EM*, p. 90)

Philosophy is required to go 'beyond itself' (Kompridis 2006, p. 52). Its task is to use ordinary language and imagery creatively, so as to represent what, either contingently or necessarily, exceeds representation – to fuse the productive and reproductive imagination so as to increase understanding – although the likelihood of it ever succeeding is highly remote. Murdoch is offering a realistic conception of philosophy's task, for not only are expectations of a 'full understanding and precise description' impracticable, they are also inappropriate (there are times 'when understanding *ought* to be withheld').

The virtues faith and hope are typically associated with religion. Murdoch says that they 'have their place' in philosophy too. They recommend an orientation towards the task of philosophizing: a preparedness to carry on with the acceptance that, as described by Kompridis, 'philosophy risks making a fool of itself, looking comical, undermining its credibility as a rational enterprise'; it 'may find itself on unfamiliar terrain where it moves awkwardly, and speaks without its customary authority' (Kompridis 2006, p. 52). Philosophy speaks with 'customary authority' when it knows what to say and, perhaps more importantly, how to say it. If philosophy is to extend 'the limits of the language' then it needs to give up its hold on customary authority, no matter how pristine or reassuring such authority is found to be. The question of philosophy's authority is always open in that it is always working out what to say and how to say it. Its role, aptly described by Kompridis, is that of the child or student – both of them designated by their role as second speakers. He writes that 'From the position of the respondent, philosophy discovers that the nature of its business is not determined by it alone, but rather, by something that it (willingly, receptively) inherits, as a child inherits a language and culture' (Kompridis 2006, p. 52).

The philosopher, like the child, frequently chooses without understanding in the very process of trying to understand. The point of the comparison is not to suggest that philosophy must overcome its naïve immaturity in order to develop into a more mature science or field of expertise (adulthood). Rather, there is something to be said for the child's perspective: being responsive to, and educated by, what is new and eludes understanding; being entranced by the sheer presence of existence rather than having merely an authoritative grasp of it; experiencing the spirit of frustration and joy coupled in the one moment; cherishing the familiar as bounded by and vulnerable to the unfamiliar; and having a willingness to begin again. These are some of the qualities that Murdoch attributes to philosophy, informed by an understanding of its imaginative character, aspirations and limits.

Murdoch, concerned to pre-empt and deflect criticisms that a philosophy of the third way will involve a 'breakdown of communication . . . condone slackness and at worst encourage violence', is emphatic that it 'is not mysticism but recognition of difficulty' (*EM*, p. 90; *MGM*, p. 236). She is not claiming that reality is ephemeral and ineffable. She is highlighting a difficulty inherent in any speaking: namely, its essential ambiguity. The metaphorical character of philosophy entails that any final utterance remains 'open to a degree of (carefully situated) ambiguity: which may in itself be a philosophical position' (*MGM*, p. 236).

Philosophical theories have the status of being complete, form-giving wholes that are unavoidably broken, inherently limited and incomplete. Human beings 'yearn for the Transcendent, for God for something divine and good and pure, but in picturing the transcendent we transform it into idols which we then realize to be contingent particulars, just things among others here below' (*MGM*, p. 56). Metaphysical pictures are idols, imperfect approximations to the truth, and so never final or complete (*MGM*, p. 84). Philosophical closure is a necessary condition for the possibility of conceptual understanding. Nevertheless it is ultimately contingent and, therefore, contestable. To an extent it falsifies reality. God and 'the various metaphysical substitutes for God – Reason, Science, History – are false deities' (*SG*, p. 79). It is an 'empirical fact' about human beings that they cannot give a full or truthful account of reality. This refers to our '"fallen" human condition' (*SG*, p. 28). Our fallen human condition is not a cause for hopelessness (there is no reason for us to try to depict reality) but a measured pessimism (depictions will be limited).

Murdoch's definition of philosophy as involving the recognition of a difficulty is important for two reasons. First, she holds that mysticism is counterproductive: instead of securing the transcendent from false idolization, as is its intention, mysticism effectively theorizes the transcendent away. For, as Murdoch explains, 'if we destroy these idols in order to reach something untainted and pure, what we really need, the thing itself, we render the Divine ineffable, and as such in peril of being judged non-existent. Then the sense of the Divine vanishes in the attempt to preserve it' (*MGM*, p. 56). If human beings refrain from describing reality, no matter how imperfect their descriptions, then human communities will probably lose the concepts that serve as reminders of its existence. Although our descriptions of reality are ultimately illusory, they keep the dream of reality alive and, in so doing, provide understanding and insight. To forget about reality's existence is to lose its power of illumination, and instruction through experience. The 'final demand or absolute is not itself a form of a life, though as an object of love it can inspire (true) life' (*MGM*, p. 145). Hence Murdoch comments that 'in order to teach, to persuade, to explain, they must talk' (*MGM*, p. 126).

Second, although it is impossible to inhabit a general truth, this fact cannot replace old 'imperfect truths' as the new meta-truth. To infer this is to make a category mistake.[10] It is a failure to recognize the profound orientation of truth-seeking that binds human beings to these inevitably, imperfect truths. Murdoch writes that 'While our motives and abilities to grasp and express truth differ, the conception of true and false is essential to human life, which without it would perish and go to ruin' (*MGM*, p. 211).[11] Human beings do not pursue the imperfect truths because of an exaggerated conception of their own epistemic powers or capacities; they pursue imperfect truths because they yearn to know what it is all about. Of this fundamental principle Murdoch says simply 'well it is so' (*MGM*, p. 55).

That philosophical theories express 'a particular value judgment in the guise of a theory', need not entail that philosophers are freely choosing the values (*SG*, p. 2). 'This is just the equation' that Murdoch is objecting to (*SG*, p. 44). She argues that some value-judgements are more compelling than others. We know this in the case of art because we 'worship the artists who we understand and enjoy, and there are few matters about which we are more uncritical and opinionated than our own aesthetic prejudices, which can combine great subjective certainty with an absence of conclusive argument' (*MGM*, p. 8). We are convinced that their art shows 'what is nearest, what is deeply and obviously true but usually invisible' (*MGM*, p. 90). Their art is porous: fictional but truthful. It opens us to a reality that we might not have otherwise recognized, 'condensing and clarifying the world' (*MGM*, p. 8). It is art that can 'enlarge our field of vision' by appealing to and accommodating certain 'musts' in human experience. Philosophy is the same.

The analogy with art raises the epistemic difficulty of how we can know which philosophical theories are more truthful: just because an individual finds a philosophical theory compelling does not make that philosophical theory true. For our conceptions of reality, no matter how seemingly scientific or neutral, are inextricable from human consciousness. The epistemic difficulty also presents a moral difficulty because philosophical theories satisfy deep emotional needs, egoistic in character. Murdoch gives the appeal of determinism as an example. She identifies Heidegger's concept of Being and Derrida's theory of language as 'new forms of determinism' (*MGM*, p. 190). She argues that we find these theories appealing because they satisfy 'a deep human wish: "to *give up*, to get rid of freedom, responsibility, remorse, all sorts of personal individual unease, and surrender to fate and the relief of it could not be otherwise"' (*MGM*, p. 190).

An individual is going to have to overcome these deep psychological needs if she is to evaluate a philosophical theory justly. In surmounting her own needs for consolation and self-aggrandizement, the individual can 'see through' a philosophical theory as a veiled rationalization, or a comforting and unifying story designed to protect individuals from reality. The less psychologically efficacious a philosophical theory is, the more likely an individual will be able to evaluate it. Of course there is no science for how to do this and it is made even more difficult by the egoistic character of human psychology. There is no means by which human beings can transcend consciousness in order to determine its orientation: egoistic fantasizing or creative imagining. We must work within it. To summarize: the epistemic question of how it is possible to know whether a philosophical theory is true is reformulated as a moral question about whether, and to what extent, a philosophical theory serves our profound egoism. It is in answering the moral question that we resolve the epistemic question.

It follows that some philosophical theories will serve as guides to morality: those theories that fill in 'a systematic explanatory background' or provide 'rich and fertile conceptual schemes', helping us to understand ourselves, our moral progress and failures 'and the reasons for the divergence of one moral temperament from another' (*SG*, p. 45). Our relationship to these philosophical theories is ultimately one of trust. We trust that the philosophical theories we find most compelling are truthful, or at least worthy of further study. The primary evidence for this coincidence will be love. Worthy philosophical theories will inspire love, as opposed to ambition, grandeur, desire, greed, avarice, jealousy and envy, for example, and transform consciousness through its reorientation. Murdoch explains that the object of our love 'enables us to look without sin upon a sinful world. It renders innocent and transforms into truthful vision our baser energies connected with power, curiosity, envy and sex' (*MGM*, p. 8). Although she is talking here about great art she thinks it is applicable to great philosophy. 'Great art inspires because it is separate, it is for nothing, it is for itself' (*MGM*, p. 8).

Murdoch concludes that as the transformational clues for philosophy are the same as those for art and ordinary consciousness, it becomes, not only legitimate but, necessary to consider whether a philosophical theory 'calms and invigorates', 'purifies our feelings' and 'unifies emotion and intellect' (*MGM*, p. 8). It is important to examine the kind of 'philosopher' or 'reader' created by a philosophical theory. This is not a matter of understanding how the theory explains philosophy; rather it is a matter of how the reader of the theory is changed through her relationship to it, i.e. what she becomes; what is learned. 'The question of truth', Murdoch writes, 'is learnt in every kind of human activity' (*MGM*, p. 418). As George Steiner observes, 'where Hegel sets Master and Servant at the core of phenomenology, Iris Murdoch places the teacher and the taught, the guru and the adept. Here the "don" and the artist are fused' (*EM*, p. xi).

It is because philosophical completeness and incompleteness are inevitable that for Murdoch the task of philosophy is to proclaim 'its own incompleteness' by way of its completeness; to acknowledge formlessness in form; to create a circle that is broken, to create a unity that admits of transcendent dis-unity (*MGM*, p. 88). A 'philosophy of the third way' requires philosophers to encounter the 'outside' of their philosophical concepts in the very process of formulating their 'inside' meaning. It acknowledges limits and accounts for exclusions because the exclusions provide both a perspective on the incompleteness of a philosophical theory or system and the impetus for reconstruction. Murdoch's 'philosophy of the third way' is intended to give meaning to the truth-seeking endeavour even though 'we have no guarantee of reaching, or a foolproof criterion for recognizing, *although we know well enough in what direction it lies*', as she writes of Sartre (*SRR*, p. 124; emphasis added).

A philosophical theory demonstrates fidelity by acknowledging its own incompleteness and normativity.[12] It 'has built in the notion of a necessary fallibility' (*SG*, p. 23). Philosophy achieves this by way of its philosophical and literary form. Again art provides an instructive analogue. For 'the work of art may seem to be a limited whole enclosed in a circle, but because of contingency and the muddled nature of the world and imperfections of language the circle is always broken' (*MGM*, p. 88). This is particularly so in the case of tragedy. According to Murdoch, tragedy is 'a broken whole' because in it 'the concluding process of the idle egoistic mind' is checked (*MGM*, p. 104). By checking egoism, tragedy intimates mortality, limitation and contingency 'as a source of energy, understanding and joy' (*MGM*, p. 87–8). It expands 'consciousness and teaches us to live inside it' (*MGM*, p. 87–8). It is in tragedy's restraint of the unifying impulse of consciousness that the reader is placed 'as it were, right up against it; close to a real awareness of death, of the senseless rubble aspect of human life which is concealed under grand illusory names such as fate, destiny, history, providence' (*MGM*, p. 104). Tragedy resists the consolation of a complete narrative so as to represent 'contingent moral existence held in a clear gaze' (*MGM*, p. 140). This is achieved through an aesthetic and moral discipline. It reveals a consciousness that has overcome its deepest psychological needs so as to 'survey complex or horrible things which would otherwise appall us' (*MGM*, p. 8). These include 'accident and contingency and the general muddle of life, the limitations of time and the discursive intellect' (*MGM*, p. 8).

Stephen Mulhall also argues that Murdoch's philosophy aspires to a harmonization of completeness and incompleteness, although he formulates it somewhat differently. According to Mulhall, Murdoch argues that philosophy must be balanced between a denial of unity or wholeness, on the one hand, and an exaggeration of unity or wholeness, on the other. Denial, he writes, 'would amount to a failure to acknowledge the independent reality of world and self', and 'exaggeration would amount to a failure to recognize that their unity, insofar as it is finite, is limited' (Mulhall 1997, p. 229). If philosophy is going to do justice to the ambiguity of our human condition then it must achieve visions and texts that reflect their own provisional nature – that realize themselves as necessarily subject to opacities, conflicts and insufficiencies that are inherent in all such theories. It must become like great art by bringing to 'our reluctant attention' the 'dense textures of the self and the material world ... that defy any final or absolute subsumption' (Mulhall 1997, p. 229). In Mulhall's terms, Murdoch asserts her vision at the same time as she focuses 'our attention to the limits or horizon of her vision, to intimations that it cannot fully accommodate, and that should therefore encourage us to begin the task of modifying, refining and otherwise appropriating the lessons it aims to teach' (p. 238).

'Philosophy of the third way' does not entail a repudiation of the search for truth, but rather an insistence on its infinite perfectibility – the existence of an ideal limit 'which always recedes' (*SG*, p. 28). As Mulhall writes, 'since every attained image of moral unity is haunted by a deeper or more truthful one, it must be regarded as provisional or illusory' (1997, p. 227). For Murdoch, reality is 'magnetic but inexhaustible' (*SG*, p. 42). She cautions that the word 'reality' 'may be used as a philosophical term provided its limitations are understood', namely that it is 'non-empirical without being in the grand sense systematic' (*SG*, p. 40). Murdoch accepts both that any account of reality is an approximation and that it is imperative for human beings to continue giving such accounts. She offers 'a calm reflective realism about morals' that is uniquely differentiated from within the parameters of a broken totality. Murdoch understands her philosophy as finite and limited in its aspiration to answer to a reality that is infinite and transcendent. It is an exercise of reason modified by the appreciation of reason's inherent imperfection. Hence Murdoch's philosophical texts do not announce themselves 'as pictures of their own accomplishments', rather they are 'stills' or 'snapshots' of a philosophy that is perpetually 'on the move' (cited in Eldridge 2001, p. 194).

Chapter 2

Reading Murdoch: Literary Form and Philosophical Precedents

Introduction

In Chapter 1 I introduced Murdoch's philosophy of the third way as based on a conception of philosophy as a 'limited whole' or 'broken totality' with ambiguity as its essential limit: the productive (expressive) and reproductive (mimetic) aspects of philosophy are inextricably intertwined (*SRR*, p. 113), The threat for philosophy conceived thus is that it will overlook or resolve this ambiguity by representing theory as either exclusively mimetic (quasi-factual) or exclusively expressive (theoretical). Philosophies of the third way are self-consciously metaphorical and entail 'a pedagogy of limits'[1]. In this chapter I argue that Murdoch's conception of her philosophy as a 'limited whole' is reflected in the literary form of both her major philosophical texts, although they do differ stylistically. I highlight three defining features: her consistent acknowledgement of temperament as the 'home' of philosophical theory, her use of ironical juxtaposition and the spirit of dialogical responsiveness that informs her work. In the second section of the chapter, I show how Murdoch reads the great romantics – Plato and Kant – as philosophers of the third way through a hermeneutic designation of their philosophies as 'religious'.

The literary dimensions of Murdoch's philosophical writing

Murdoch consistently argues that philosophers miss the point if they assume that metaphysical theories persuade by virtue of being logically self sufficient. Philosophers must not be seduced into believing that the impersonality of philosophy (its theoretical and conceptual nature) allows it to transcend the personal 'I' (contingent, historical and affective) and offer a final and complete description of reality as if viewed from an uninvolved observer's perspective. Such a description is impossible on Murdoch's view, and she reminds her readers that philosophical theories are erected by individuals. Their purpose is to give life and existence a unifying form in much the same way as concepts, and, as with concepts, the intelligibility of these theories depends on their ability to alleviate deep psychological needs and speak to our most profound convictions.

The imperatives for philosophical theorizing are as follows. First, philosophical theories need to be checked 'against what we know of human nature' through 'ordinary (non-theorized, non-jargonized) views of it' in order for it to protect itself from our egoistic tendencies (*MGM*, p. 216). As human nature is the unmistaken context for philosophizing (even the most technical), philosophers are reliant on the social sciences – anthropology, psychology and sociology – for information about how human beings operate. It is important, however, that these views be 'ordinary' and not distorted by scientism (i.e. that the discipline should not model itself on a positivistic conception of science). Murdoch enlists the work of Sigmund Freud as telling a story about what human beings are like. Although the social sciences are important on Murdoch's view, their relevance to philosophy is ultimately subject to the phenomenological descriptions of what individuals, 'I's, experience life to be like. The humanities, in particular literature and visual art, remain paramount.

Second, philosophers must develop strategies to keep narcissistic delusions of omniscience in check and to acknowledge inherent limitations and incompleteness. These strategies include knowing oneself and knowing humanity. It is important for the philosopher to know how she fantasizes herself and who she is, in order to be able to consider and evaluate her own philosophizing against such a self-understanding. This self-understanding is helped by going to literature, art and the social sciences as the vehicles for learning about human nature. Another strategy is to experiment with different rhetorical styles in the search for a philosophical speaking and writing that is less closed and more open, less a monologue and more dialogical, less defensive and more invitation, and less conclusive and more inconclusive. A further strategy is to take seriously the criticisms of others, not as bars to a theory's success but as insights into its limitations, prejudices, idiosyncrasies and blind-spots.

Murdoch not only appeals to these imperatives and strategies in her conception of philosophy. She exemplifies them in the development of her philosophizing and philosophical writings, as I aim to demonstrate in the following three sections: temperament, irony and dialogue.

Temperament

Temperament is a term that Murdoch uses and, as it is rather old-fashioned, we are more likely to associate it with 'being temperamental', that is, a susceptibility to fits of excitable or moody behaviour – this provides a clue but not the full meaning of 'temperament'. Temperament refers to an individual's nature as it contributes to her behaviour. Other terms in Murdoch's lexicon used to refer to the same phenomenon include 'personality' and 'historical individuality'. These terms refer to the origins of an individual's actions that encompass, far in excess of reasons, national and personal history, political affiliation, personality type, the interrupting traumatic events, enforced roles, predilections and fantasies. Though largely contingent and historical, an individual's personality or temperament governs behaviour, shapes identity and informs the individual's relationship to their own becoming.

In Murdoch's view, individuals are constrained but not wholly determined by temperament. Individuals can take more or less responsibility for their temperament and, in the process, partially liberate or further succumb to its tyranny. Taking responsibility for one's temperament involves, in the first place, recognizing it. Recognition is neither easy nor straightforward, as Murdoch's fictional characters reveal – although she borrows from Freud, Murdoch consistently denies that there can be an objective psychological or sociological science of analysis. If an individual is able provisionally to identify her temperament, this does not ensure that she will be able to change it, or indeed know how to go about changing it. (Of course, sometimes, fortuitously, something happens – generally an accident – to cause a person to act in a new way.)

Murdoch is not a confessional writer and rarely describes her own temperament, but she does reference temperament with the view to reminding others (readers and philosophers) of the need for introspection as a necessary condition for the possibility of truth. In her earliest philosophical work, *The Sovereignty of Good*, Murdoch acknowledges her own temperament as a permanent background condition for how she is moved to respond to an argument and what she *is* compelled to argue for. The following examples demonstrate how Murdoch refers to temperament to qualify her philosophical arguments: 'one feels impelled to say something like' (*SG*, p. 23); 'temperament will play its part in determining whether or not we *want* to attack or whether we are content. I am not content' (*SG*, p. 16); 'one seems to be relentlessly prevented from saying something which one is irresistibly impelled to say' (*SG*, p. 21); and 'one feels here, live and kicking in the tired modern soul, burdened by all sorts of abstract and scientific theorizing, the indignation of Kierkegaard against Hegel' (*MGM*, p. 202).

In the later work, *Metaphysics as a Guide to Morals*, she has less need for these kinds of qualifications (for reasons that I will explain presently), and so she makes the point in general terms. She states explicitly that 'problems are set up in philosophy with ulterior motives', and refers to herself as a case in point (*MGM*, p. 171). Although she feels that what she has to say is philosophically significant, it is likely that the only reason she believes consciousness to be a discussable problem is because she wants 'consciousness or self-being' to be 'the fundamental mode or form of moral being' (*MGM*, p. 171).

On the basis of her assumption that it is a philosopher's convictions that drive philosophical theorizing, and not the other way round, Murdoch concludes that it is incumbent on philosophers and their readers periodically to 'stand back and ask: Well, what *am* I worried about, and what do I want, what am I after, what is supposed to be missing' (*MGM*, p. 238)? In other words, it is important to probe 'a philosopher's motives' in order to ascertain what psychological needs are being served by the philosophical theory (*MGM*, p. 50). Murdoch is not reductionist in her use of psychology, for she thinks of psychology and temperament in only a very general sense, and not a scientifically detailed or psychoanalytical sense (*MGM*, p. 50). Identifying the psychological incentives for a theory is a significant hermeneutical strategy because these motivations are typically unconscious and unrecognizable.

Discovery of the deep psychological impulses that at one end inform and the other end govern philosophical theorizing has an ambiguous status. In some cases the discovery is a cause for continued, more deferential, enquiry. Discovering the theory's psychological foundation gives the critic a reason to take it seriously and analyse it in greater depth. Plato would be a case in point: it is because his philosophy expresses 'our certainty that goodness is something indubitably real, unitary, and (somehow) simple' that we are compelled to understand it more fully (*EM*, p. 408). The philosophy is thought to contain a justification for the psychological well-spring that it speaks to and engenders. As Murdoch states, a 'naïve reaction needs to be philosophically justified' (*MGM*, p. 202). The discovery of a theory's deep psychological source can be cause for suspicion too: it is a reason to abandon the theory or at least question the root cause of its persuasiveness. Murdoch, echoing Wittgenstein, warns that 'the fact that one is irresistibly impelled to say [something] need not mean that anything *else* is the case' (*SG*, p. 21).

Whether the discovery results in enquiry or suspicion depends on the type of psychological impulse identified. Although discerning actual psychological impulses is difficult, differentiating between them is not – Murdoch has an uncomplicated view of what constitutes good and bad psychologies. A good psychology allows for moral self-improvement. It reflects the individual's desire to be 'touched' by a higher power, i.e. to receive a sacrament (a source of good energy). A philosophical theory will support this good psychology if it provides the conceptual space for desiring genuine

Reading Murdoch: Literary Form and Philosophical Precedents 41

self-improvement. Instead of encouraging moral self-improvement, bad psychologies are sado-masochistic; they have the appearance of chastizing the ego but effectively indulge and inflame it.[2] A philosophical theory will support this bad psychology if it allows us to feel better about ourselves in the acknowledgment of egoistic deviancy and perversion. Murdoch describes it as follows:

> One's self is interesting, so one's motives are interesting, and the unworthiness of one's motives is interesting. Fascinating too is the alleged relation of master to slave, of the good self to the bad self which, oddly enough, ends in such curious compromises. (Kafka's struggle with the devil which ends up in bed). (*SG*, p. 68)

Irony[3]

'Irony' is not part of Murdoch's lexicon, and it is not a concept that she develops. I am using it here in an ordinary, non-technical sense.[4] Murdoch cannot be said to have a philosophy of irony, and yet it is possible to read irony in her philosophical writings. She uses irony, or more accurately adopts an ironical stance towards her own philosophy as ultimately uncertain, and this is reflected in her tone and the many playful ways in which she destabilizes the asserted truth of her claims and anticipates their limits. Irony is an acknowledgement, within the theory, that the necessity of its apparent 'finality' precludes the possibility of its ever being true. Irony is not premised on the ability of the philosopher to specify the limits of her philosophy, for the ironist-philosopher need not know them. Irony is not a judgement based on actual discerned limitations, but is more like a creed of faith: it is based on a view about philosophy's incompleteness even though that incompleteness may not be always and everywhere apparent.

Having assumed the necessary fallibility of her philosophy, the ironist-philosopher will be vigilant in her efforts to ascertain the limits of her theory.[5] She will demonstrate a hypercritical attitude towards different philosophical theories (including her own) and to the philosophical enterprise over all. It follows that the ironist-philosopher does not eschew serious and sustained enquiry but engages in the enquiry on the understanding that it has no absolute endpoint, only contingent ones. This is likely to be reflected in an ironical or playful distancing from the conclusions of the enquiry; an almost neurotic second-guessing by the ironist-philosopher; and a more than tokenistic interest in alternative theories. The ironist-philosopher is subject to the explanatory framework but also transcends it through the recognition of the framework as inherently limited. The ironist-philosopher escapes the work of philosophy at certain key points intimating her larger existence as embodied, historical, daughter, mother and friend – the deliberate confusion of art and life is a form of ironical protest (*MGM*, p. 22).

Murdoch employs irony to signal the incompleteness underlying all philosophical theorizing. Although appearing to argue for a 'final' vocabulary, she uses irony to remind the reader that there can be no such 'final' vocabulary – philosophy has no endpoint; no resolute conclusion. Murdoch uses irony in two ways: the interplay between philosophical and religious language, and the interplay of philosophical and religious language with the ordinary and everyday. The teasing interplay of philosophical and religious language and imagery – her comparison of Heidegger with Lucifer and Socrates with Jesus Christ, for example – may appear natural to some, but many readers will find it conspicuous. It is intended to undermine the epistemic presumptuousness of philosophy and religion, blending their languages back into ordinary speech – Murdoch challenges the legitimacy of our so-called need to invent new and separate languages. It is here that she reveals her Wittgensteinian influences, for she is not so much interested in words as in the determination of their significance through use.

Murdoch conceives of language as a vehicle for human consciousness. It is, in the words of Maria Antonaccio, 'an instrument of the individual's knowledge and the world' (Antonaccio 2000, p. 90). Murdoch, in the interests of human community and communication, consciously resists and deconstructs specialized philosophical and religious languages. This is because they are comprehensible only to small groups of individuals, and so imply that religious and philosophical understanding is equally 'specialized'. Murdoch emphatically states that to be human *is* to participate in the search for religious and philosophical understanding – this defines what it means to be human and is an integral part of her naturalism. She accepts as fact that individuals 'go on knowing' irrespective of whether the metaphysical or theological apparatus is present. The reason that she describes the void as such a threat to our humanity is precisely because it jeopardizes our grasp of the possibility for meaning (*MGM*, pp. 498–503).

In the case of philosophy, Murdoch's irony serves to highlight and question the discipline's sense of itself as a privileged, more scientific, mode of enquiry. She hints at philosophy's shared mythical status with religion by alluding to its 'patron saints', in Hume and Kant, and its moral pilgrims (*SG*, pp. 26, 92); its concepts, like attention, that serve as 'our daily bread' (*SG*, p. 44); that an argumentative defence is 'a hymn of praise in gratitude for the joys and consolations' of it (*MGM*, p. 8); and that some philosophy is 'positively Luciferian' (*SG*, p. 72).[6] On a more serious note, Murdoch draws on such religious terminology as 'original sin,' 'humility', 'redemption', 'grace' and 'sacrament', to name the central concepts of her philosophy. She does not directly import their religious sense, choosing instead to rely on a deep resonance of philosophical and religious meaning. Although they serve as technical terms in her philosophy, Murdoch does not so much define them as allow them to fall into place: readers who are religiously inclined or trained will know what she means by virtue of association, and those who are not can work it out from the text. But is the religious sense of these terms adequate for understanding Murdoch's philosophy? Do we really know what Murdoch means by humility, for example? Is the substitution of good for God, a clue?

Murdoch's employment of religious terminology, in the naming of her key philosophical concepts, is designed to challenge the presumption of religious privilege. Her point is that religions do not have a monopoly on concepts such as sin, humility, grace for reasons to do with their theological apparatus, nor are they necessarily the best guides to what these concepts mean. There is a wealth of conceptual resources in psychology, art, physics, economics and philosophy because concepts such as sin, humility, grace and redemption are an inextricable part of the structure of consciousness. Murdoch's point is that questions such as, 'Are human beings flawed and what are the possible sources for redemption?', are worked through, continuously, across the disciplines, from science, to psychology, to art, and by individuals in ordinary day-to-day life.

Murdoch argues against believing that to speak personally is to speak autobiographically; personal insights can be articulated philosophically and religiously. Although these languages appear to be speaking from the God's eye (or scientific) perspective, they in effect articulate an individual's sense of the whole of life. It is for this reason that she utilizes the ironical interplay of philosophical and religious language with the 'ordinary and everyday'. It identifies this 'two-way movement' as an 'abiding and not a regrettable characteristic' of philosophy and religion (*SG* p. 17). Murdoch illustrates this 'two-way movement' with the following example: 'McTaggart says that time is unreal, Moore replies that he has just had his breakfast' (*SG*, p. 1). Although Moore's retort is humorous, Murdoch cautions readers not to miss the seriousness of its intent. If philosophical theorizing is to be meaningful for us as human beings then it must be rooted in, and answerable to, ordinary, everyday human existence. It must be possible for a moral philosophy to be 'inhabited'. As Murdoch sketches her 'metaphysical theory' she mentions obvious, simple facts about us. She mentions a mother and daughter-in-law (*SG*, p. 17); 'housework and all kinds of nameless "unskilled" fixing or cleanings or arrangings' (*MGM*, p. 180); nursery rhymes (*SG*, p. 28); paying bills (*SG*, p. 36); sweeping the floor and 'other small everyday acts' (*SG*, p. 43); 'people who bring home potted plants and watch kestrels' (*SG*, p. 85); 'forms of mud, hair and dirt' (*SG*, p. 88); falling in love; and learning languages.

She also considers such questions as

> Should a retarded child be kept at home or sent to an institution? Should an elderly relation who is a trouble-maker be cared for or asked to go away? Should an unhappy marriage be continued for the sake of the children? Should I leave my family in order to do political work? Should I neglect them in order to practise my art (*SG*, p. 91)?

Murdoch plays here with the epistemic and moral presumption of both philosophy and religion as being utterly distinct from, and superior to, ordinary consciousness and life. The commonplace, as she points out, is not as mundane as it first appears. Day-to-day living is filled with great seriousness, significant enquiry, high drama, poignancy and beauty. It is frequently animated by the aspiration to do justice to a transcendent value that claims us from a position of beyond. The mother who is deciding whether or not a retarded child should be kept at home is trying to determine what love means. She is working out what it is for her to love this child as she works out what it is for her to love her family – all in light of her understanding of what love is. The decision of whether or not a retarded child should be kept at home is both a conceptual and practical problem – the two are mutually informing and cannot be prised apart.

Murdoch's intention for these various and playful juxtapositions is serious. She wants her readers to become disoriented so that they can begin to deconstruct their preconceptions about where they derive meaning and what the sources of truth are. Human beings do not learn from one discipline, one thinker, one art form or even an artist – learning has its source in both the lowest and the highest dimensions of human experience and culture. Her argument is that philosophical theory and religious doctrine are both formulated articulations of learning and, as such, have their origins in those experiences that claim us and inspire us to think beyond the limits of our conceptual understanding. These experiences that claim us can come from anywhere. Examples include: walking with one's child to the bus-stop in the morning, waiting in a queue, sharing a meal with family, having coffee with a friend, reading in bed with one's lover, swimming in the ocean and hearing Beethoven's Ninth Symphony. Properly understood, philosophical theory and religious doctrine cannot replace what they propose to account for, namely the many and varied sacraments (sources of good energy).

Dialogue

If irony and references to temperament signal the incompleteness of a philosophical theory, then modifying the theory as a response to others' reactions, signals the primacy of its search for truth. Others' reactions (affirmation, criticism and incomprehension) are critical for a particular theory's 'truthfulness'. If, as Murdoch assumes, there is no route from within the operations of consciousness to its external ground – there is no science of consciousness – then we have no choice but to evaluate the insights of consciousness through dialogue with other human beings. She says that 'uses of words by persons grouped round a common object is a central and vital human activity' (*SG*, p. 32). It is principally through dialogue that individuals share and engage with one another's concepts. Murdoch gives the example of the art critic, who 'can help us if we are in the presence of the same object and if we know something about his scheme of concepts. Both contexts are relevant to our ability to move towards "seeing more", towards seeing what he sees' (*SG*, p. 32).

Dialogue is a symptom of learning and an instrument for it. Murdoch echoes the Platonic thought that it is words spoken in conversation that 'occasion wisdom' (*SG*, p. 32). It is through dialogue that individuals discover what is illuminated and obscured by particular concepts, enabling them to differentiate ones that are deep, profound and insightful from those that are superficial, unsatisfactory and corrupt. Deep concepts need not be more sophisticated, for as Murdoch rightly points out, a 'smart set of concepts may be a most efficient instrument of corruption' (*SG*, p. 33). Deep concepts are often poignantly simple, because they involve seeing what we are too busy, deluded and self-absorbed to see, like our mortality and the 'the sheer alien pointless independent existence of animals, birds and trees' (*SG*, p. 85). Instead of being a neutral activity, dialogue is the means by which individuals discover the particular limits of their own and other's concepts – as they grasp the inherent ambiguity of all concepts.

Dialogue is pedagogical and, for this reason, ultimately moral. Once individuals detect the limits of certain concepts and glimpse better ones, they are compelled to accommodate what they have learned – a progress in their understanding occurs as they differentiate and dispel falsifying concepts in the search for greater truth. This progress in understanding is always accompanied by an acknowledgement of how the previous concept 'worked' by satisfying our deepest egoistic needs. A concept might provide consolation, fulfil a lack, prevent us from confronting a difficult truth, distract us from what was really at issue, or allow us better to identify with a familial, social or cultural group. We are all familiar with such developments. These developments are moral for two reasons. First, the progress in understanding involves a new containment or curtailment of the ego that was not available prior to the new concept. Second, the progress in understanding typically involves not just one but a set of concepts that, when altered, cause the individual to see many things differently, establishing a different worldview and leading them to act in different ways.

As a consequence, open, ongoing and honest conversation with diverse groups of individuals about concepts that are central and common is a necessary and critical 'checking procedure' for individuals, given their 'redefining' and 'reassessing' (*SG*, p. 26). Dialogue reveals the limits of our concepts, exposes us to better concepts, affords us the opportunity to learn and prompts us to become better individuals – if learning defines the human condition then so too does dialogue. The reader's dialogue with Murdoch's philosophical texts reveals the limits of her ideas: the degree to which they enlist and assuage Murdoch's, and our own, self-serving fantasy mechanism and the degree to which they speak of and to our humanity. Of course, our judgement may be mistaken, and there needs to be strong residual doubt about any of the ideas that appear to speak to our humanity, precisely because there is no a priori or guaranteed method by which to determine whether or not we are right, or if the distinction is sound. It is significant that if an individual feels convinced of an idea's truth, this is even more reason to bring the seemingly truthful idea into dialogue with other ideas, by engaging individuals in conversation about them. The aim is to detect traces of the surreptitious, duplicitous, self-consoling and self-aggrandizing psyche in our attraction for the idea.

Murdoch recognizes that in the tradition of both Wittgenstein and Socrates the meaning of her philosophy is as much about how others take it up as it is about anything that she says herself. She articulates this thought at the end of 'The Idea of Perfection', when she writes that her philosophical 'sketch' must be evaluated according to 'its power to connect, to illuminate, to explain, and to make new and fruitful places for reflection' (*SG*, pp. 34, 45). It is for this reason that she invites her readers to assess what she says, according to how what she says impacts their life with concepts. Readers are not to evaluate her theory according to a set of predetermined, objective set of criteria devised; rather they are invited to take her concepts of love, goodness, humility and redemption, for example, and bring them into dialogue with their own and others' concepts in an effort to determine which console and which are true.

Murdoch's dialogical relationship with her readership informs the stylistic development from *The Sovereignty of Good* to *Metaphysics as a Guide to Morals*; this development reflects the modification of her message in light of others' understanding, misinterpretation, comment and correction. For example, the arguments in *The Sovereignty of Good* are more concise and less conversational in tone than the arguments of *Metaphysics as a Guide to Morals*. Although Murdoch's purpose in *The Sovereignty of Good* is to defend the 'virtuous peasant', she accentuates her own philosophical expertise by her authoritative control of the arguments. In the later book, it seems as if Murdoch not only appreciates the prior discrepancy between her philosophical thesis and 'expert' manner of defending it, but also how 'appearing the expert' fulfilled some very deepseated psychological needs of her own. In *Metaphysics as a Guide to Morals*, she has less control over the arguments and allows her thinking to range over a vast terrain. It considers contemporary trends in art and philosophy, canonical and not-so-canonical figures in the history of philosophy, as well as contemporary social and political issues.

Murdoch's comments on Plato and Arthur Schopenhauer suggest that she deliberately changed her philosophical style. She notes that it is the literary quality of their writings that ameliorates the austerity and pessimism of their philosophical outlook. She says of Plato, that his 'remarks seem less tiresomely puritanical if we also recall the amazingly open happy sunny (Platonic metaphor) atmosphere of the dialogues and how full they are of wit and jokes' (*MGM*, p. 381). She congratulates Schopenhauer for his philosophical style: 'an insatiable omnivorous muddled cheerful often casual volubility' (*MGM*, p. 79). She compliments him on his rambling, jocular humour, and references to 'animals, insects, and fishes' (*MGM*, p. 77). His relationship with the reader is, she thinks, 'relaxed and amicable, confiding, that of a kindly teacher or fellow seeker. He tells stories and makes jokes' (*MGM*, p. 79). Most importantly, 'he is prepared to exhibit his puzzlement and to ramble', conceding the significance, magnitude and difficulty of the intellectual obstacle that he faces (*MGM*, p. 252). He 'rushes off at a tangent, tries to wander round it, talks, even chats about it' (*MGM*, p. 252).

Although Murdoch's philosophical commitments do not radically alter in the 30 years between *The Sovereignty of Good* and *Metaphysics as a Guide to Morals*, there is development of emphasis that mirrors the stylistic development. In both works Murdoch responds to the strongest voices and central preoccupations of her philosophical community at the time – existentialism, behaviourism and Wittgenstein in *The Sovereignty of Good*; and Derrida, Theodor W. Adorno, Marxism and post-structuralism in *Metaphysics as a Guide to Morals*. Always the pedagogue, Murdoch frames what she says in relationship to the concerns of her audience, so as to make her perspective relevant and meaningful – particularly as this is also a test of the perspective's inherent meaningfulness. So, the first book addresses conscious and unconscious adherents of existentialism (with its emphasis on human freedom), whereas the later book addresses the conscious and unconscious adherents of post-structuralism (with its emphasis on how language constructs subjectivity). In Murdoch's view, whereas existentialism exaggerates the subject's freedom by erroneously tying it to the will, post-structuralism nullifies subjective freedom by subordinating it to the greater determinism of language.

Murdoch offers *Metaphysics as a Guide to Morals* as a rejoinder to established interpretations of her earlier work, *The Sovereignty of Good*. Whereas *The Sovereignty of Good* focuses on love and the unexamined life, *Metaphysics as a Guide to Morals* focuses on the imaginatively unifying activity of consciousness, its expression in artistic endeavour, and the paradigmatic status of art with respect to human endeavour. *The Sovereignty of Good* is informed by Murdoch's abiding concern – a concern inspired by G.E. Moore and his Cambridge disciples – that she should not appear to represent all human experience as aesthetic. Murdoch is loath to defend hedonism or to offer an aesthetic definition of the Good. She does not write of art in order to elevate artistic consciousness above the messiness of ordinary consciousness. Her aim is to do justice to the inevitability, muddled ordinariness and depth of morality by reference to art and the aesthetic.[7] Although Murdoch touches on art and aesthetics in *The Sovereignty of Good*, she makes it the centerpiece of her argument in *Metaphysics as a Guide to Morals*, having become more confident in her ability to discuss aesthetics and art without appearing to privilege it above human experience.

Timeliness and increased confidence are only part of the explanation for Murdoch's philosophizing about art and aesthetics in *Metaphysics as a Guide to Morals*. Her intention is to correct a popular misrepresentation of her philosophical position as a situational or caring ethics, ensuing from her earlier focus on love and the unexamined life. In *Metaphysics as a Guide to Morals*, she is far less ambivalent about conventional morality. She defends the necessity of attention, duties and axioms, arguing that individuals do not have 'to choose between "attention" and "duty", we live with both' (*MGM*, p. 220).[8] They do 'not have to choose between activism and inwardness or feel that one is bound to swallow the other' (*MGM*, p. 362). The concept of duty, she argues, is of 'greatest importance' because it expresses 'our sense of the absolute nature of moral obligation' (*MGM*, p. 384). To recognize oneself as subject to duty, just *is* to recognize oneself as a moral subject. 'The idea of a network of ordinary duties is an extremely important aspect of morals, it goes with a sense of being always on duty, a conscript and not a gentleman volunteer' (*MGM*, p. 383).

Murdoch defends duty as the most obvious moral experience. Duties are, she argues, much more flexible than philosophers would have us believe, as they admit of many formulations from those of the greatest generality to the most specific. Duties introduce 'order and calm' and help us in 'the formation of moral habits': they define certain acts as unambiguously moral, so that when individuals consistently perform those actions they internalize the relevant moral principles (*MGM*, p. 494). Axioms, as Murdoch uses the term, refer to political thinking and decision-making. Axioms make our moral thinking amenable to the political process. Axioms operate like duties: 'as a battle flag or as a barrier' (*MGM*, p. 356). They have the power to galvanize individuals into moral action or, conversely, to prevent them from acting immorally. Attention, duty and axioms are interrelated and interreliant, although not without certain tension. Over all they 'know their roles, and places, and when they have rights against each other' and are each necessary for 'a realistic view of morality' (*MGM*, p. 362).

In summary, Murdoch's conception of philosophy of the 'third way' is reflected in the literary qualities of her philosophical style, the appeals to temperament, the use of ironical juxtaposition and the spirit of dialogical responsiveness that animates her work. In the next section I argue that her conception of philosophy extends to her interpretations of the 'religious philosophies' of Plato and Kant.

The 'religious' philosophies of Plato and Kant

Murdoch acknowledges that her interpretations of Plato and Kant are atypical and that she is not unduly worried about this. She recognizes that her analysis works against the literal-mindedness dominant in analytic philosophy – a literal-mindedness that has, she thinks, caused analytic philosophers to misunderstand and misjudge Plato. The literal-mindedness stems from the mistaken belief that the first principle of philosophy is to establish a complete separation between fact and value. Assuming that humans access the facts by way of science, analytic philosophy aligns itself with scientific methodology in an effort to distance itself from the religious production of pictorial and narrative expressions of value. Analytic philosophy fails to appreciate that the picture of reality as inherently 'factual' or 'scientific' is itself a picture, expressive of certain values and, as a result, psychologically instrumental.

If the assumed separation of fact and value is just another value-laden depiction of reality and our relationship to it, then values and pictures may be far harder to escape than analytic philosophers would have us believe. So, just as analytic philosophy would have us abandon the quaintness of religious story-telling in favour of the superiority of its scientific methodology, Murdoch is returning us to the very mythical, picturesque and redemptive qualities of religion that analytic philosophy seeks so hard to deny. She wants her readers to see that 'some great philosophical pictures are also great religious pictures, and illustrate how closely philosophy and theology can come to each other, while still wisely apart' (*MGM*, p. 56).

It is in light of this return that Murdoch is able to interpret the analytic adherence to the fact/value distinction as the expression of a deep commitment to truth – that our relationship to truth be invulnerable to either scepticism or relativism. Murdoch sympathizes with the analytic concern for truth and truthfulness, but considers the assumed separation of fact and value as a misconceived way of going about it. This is because it ignores the ways in which our evaluative vocabulary and orientation involves the individual in truth-seeking knowledge and the discipline of desire. Values entail truth because the desire to value only what *is* truly valuable is internal to human valuing. In other words, individuals change their values in light of what they learn to be more or less valuable. They want to get values right just as they want to get things right grammatically and mathematically. It is because human beings have values that they desire to be right about them; they want to achieve 'truth instead of falsehood, reality instead of appearance' (*MGM*, p. 39).

If the separation of fact and value is a picture of reality that aspires to preserve us in our relationship to truth, from either scepticism or relativism, then Murdoch's point simply is that analytic philosophers are mistaken if they think this is the only, or even the best, means of doing so. For example, it is not Murdoch's intention to diminish truth in her relegation of philosophy to the creation, analysis, rejection and re-creation of pictures. Rather, she wishes to reveal the necessity, complex character and ambiguous negotiation of truth that occurs in the human inhabitation and evaluation of these pictures – ' "Truth" is not a collection of facts' (*MGM*, p. 398). It is also intended to reveal the sheer importance of truth: discerning what is true is absolutely critical for what we value and the manner in which we pursue it. Murdoch argues that it is because truth plays such a crucial role 'in a picture of the omnipresence of morality and evaluation in human life', it would seem 'mad to begin philosophy by asserting a complete separation of fact from value, and then attempting to give a satisfactory account of morals' (*MGM*, p. 39).

Some philosophers are more aware than others of the religious timbre of their discipline; some philosophers self-consciously adopt the third way. Their philosophizing is informed by the following: consciousness of the fantastical or mythical status of their respective theory; recognition of a transcendent reality; due regard for the educative force of a theory, concept, individual or experience; an understanding of all education as moral education; and faith in the reality of the good. Murdoch identifies Plato and Kant as two such 'religious philosophers' (*MGM*, p. 50). They both allude to the inherently pictorial and magical nature of their theorizing (*MGM*, p. 43). They appreciate that their metaphysical theories are fantasies that serve as 'regulative longings' (Kneller 2006, p. 210). They are confident that their theories have some basis in reality because these theories are the result of their desire to render intelligible reality's residual trace.

The religious philosopher is, to use Jane Kneller's apt phrase, the 'noble fantast ... placed alongside Plato's philosopher gazing out of the cave, or with Rousseau, surveying the natural goodness of humanity in the state of nature, or even standing with Kant, gazing in awe at the starry heavens above' (2006, p. 210). The abstraction that Plato and Kant appear to have us escape into is an illusion designed to convey 'reality' or the non-determinate qualities of experience. Hence Plato's myth of the cave includes as much descent as there is ascent, depicting the 'noble fantast' as he seeks to inspire and compel the cave-dwellers to look beyond what they see (*MGM*, p. 318). Like the man returning to the cave, Plato and Kant do not give a literal description of reality but convey some sense of it through their description of what reality is like. Murdoch says that Plato 'cannot be said to have taken any form of myth literally and constantly draws attention to its status of an edifying or hermeneutic "as if"' (*MGM*, p. 402). Plato gives this hermeneutical quality to his philosophizing through his literary style: he writes in dialogue form, mixes up myth and argument and is self-consciously messy. It is by these means that he emphasizes the incompleteness of his 'theory' and confounds literalist interpretation. His goal is to present 'instructive *pictures*' as part of a 'hermeneutic "as if"' (*MGM*, p. 10).

If a philosophy is aware of itself as a fantastical representation that expresses what our experience of ourselves in relationship to reality is like, then reality is established as necessarily 'somewhere else, separate and sole, under the guard of dragon-like concepts' (*MGM*, p. 56). Plato's explanation is metaphorical or analogical, based on the assumption that a reality which is necessarily transcendent only appears to us 'at our own level, as an image' (*MGM*, p. 183). So, 'there is no Platonic "elsewhere", similar to the Christian "elsewhere". What is higher is, as Eckhart observed, *inside* the soul' (*MGM*, p. 399; emphasis added). As Murdoch notes, 'In fact Plato (more than any other philosopher) "saves" metaphysics by showing how the noumenal and the phenomenal exist *inside* each human life. There is nowhere else, it is all here' (*MGM*, p. 182).

Murdoch is of the view that metaphysics 'is inspired by a gifted thinker's scrutiny of his *own thought*' (*MGM*, p. 398). Because Plato and Kant give an account of 'the *internal* relation of value, truth, cognition' they prioritize human consciousness (*MGM*, p. 39; emphasis added). For while 'thought "aims" at reality', it does so with 'only varying degrees of success' (*MGM*, p. 398). 'Reality' is a normative ideal that serves as an object of thought because, logically speaking, it is difficult for an individual to think seriously about what she considers to be non-real. 'Reality' demarcates more truthful pictures from those that are less truthful – art is a useful analogy at this point.[9] Although philosophies are pictorial and reflect their origins in human consciousness, they do not share the same epistemic status, for some of them admit of more reality than others. Murdoch suggests that these metaphysical pictures serve as '*metaphysical barriers* across certain well-worn tracks into depravity' (*EM* p. 401).[10]

Professor Marije Altorf is right to emphasize the image of the 'barrier' in Murdoch's philosophy (Altorf 2008, p. 8). A barrier marks both the limit and meeting-place of the two spaces that it divides, and its purpose is to control and direct movement of whatever is on either side. Some barriers prevent access, whereas others are more porous and permit the easy movement of selective elements. Porous barriers serve as membranes or filters, as Murdoch implies through the image of the lungs. A metaphysical theory acts as a barrier to the soul, in the two senses of that term. The theory keeps reality out by picturing it; by imposing a form on what we must assume is essentially formless. Yet it also pictures something and, as with pictures in general, admits of some reality. That a theory permits reality to enter the soul is evidenced by the soul's consequent reorientation, transformation and education. Metaphysical theories are like 'ladders' in this regard (remember Wittgenstein). Comprehending the theory is analogous to ascending a ladder: the reader is taken to a new understanding by the theory/ladder, but upon arrival at this new understanding she no longer needs the theory/ladder that got her there (*MGM*, p. 318).

Murdoch reads Plato's *Republic* as being 'primarily a spiritual guidebook' for two reasons (*MGM*, p. 388). First, Plato appreciates the nature of our spiritual struggle. He describes the feeling that individuals have of moving forever closer to that which claims us but eludes our comprehension of it; he describes 'the disturbing magnetism of *truth*' and our move towards 'selfless lucidity' (*MGM*, p. 11). This lucidity is selfless because our values, and desires, are transformed by something beyond and other to our own fantasy mechanism (*MGM*, p. 11). Second, Plato's depiction of this struggle is instrumental in the struggle of his readers. It engages his readers in dialogue, acts as magnetic force, and permits them to see reality. In a way not dissimilar from art, readers discern the truth of his philosophical picture by way of its educative force – its ability to illuminate and reorient. Readers recognize its truth by way of its effect, by how it conditions and transforms consciousness. This idea is manifest in Plato's definition of moral rationality as the ability to respond to 'a transcendent source incarnate at various levels in our cognitive and emotional experience' (*MGM*, p. 56).

Murdoch acknowledges that Kant is more complex on this issue because he denies the existence of 'moral experience' or 'moral consciousness'. She thinks that it is possible to find, however, scattered throughout his philosophical writings, the critical 'intrusions of value into phenomenal awareness' (*MGM*, p. 223). It is made possible by Kant's category of the aesthetic imagination 'which is spontaneous and free and able to create a "second nature"' (*MGM*, p. 316). Murdoch thinks that this idea 'can go very far, further perhaps than the author intended', but to do so it needs to be 'let out of the small corner denoted by "fine art"' (*MGM*, p. 314). What if aesthetic imagination, as opposed to the empirical imagination, were the transcendental condition for the possibility of experience? What if phenomenal reality were structured 'by a spontaneous, creative, *free* faculty' that was not neutral but reflected our deepest imaginings and then values (*MGM*, p. 314)? What would be the significance then of Kant's 'peripheral concepts of the sublime and Respect for Law, which lead back into the phenomenal self' and in which Murdoch detects his 'softening grace' (*MGM*, p. 223)?

A more extensive discussion of the sublime is reserved for Chapters 3 and 4 of this book. For the purposes of this chapter, Murdoch perceives in Kant's concepts of the sublime and respect for the law, occasions for the differentiation between bad and good imagining. These concepts preserve the aesthetic imagination as purposeful and potentially objective by making it conceptually possible for the individual to move away from 'narrowly banal false pictures ... toward the expression and elucidation ... of what is true and deep' based on some contact with noumenal reality (*MGM*, p. 321). The sublime, for example, uniquely describes the individual's 'immediate phenomenal consciousness of moral "self-feeling"' (*MGM*, p. 223). This is significant because experience, according to Kant, is by definition phenomenal (not noumenal) which makes the sublime a liminal experience – individuals have an 'experience' of their noumenal reality. As liminal experience it directs attention to the whole of phenomenal experience as inherently limited, bringing the individual to the edge of what she finds intelligible.

As it concerns noumenal reality, the sublime cannot refer to 'an experience' in the strict sense, for to be an experience is to be subject to the empirical (Kant) or aesthetic (Murdoch) imagination. But if it is not an experience then what is it? It is, simply, an intimation of a higher order, serving to reorient and educate the individual as to how she should live out her relationship to phenomenal reality. The problem is that the status of the sublime as authoritative but non-empirical makes it susceptible to risk.

It easily degenerates into 'a pleasurable end-in-itself' – as was the case with some forms of romanticism (*MGM*, p. 223). Instead of integrating the sublime back into ordinary experience, the sublime justified not experiencing life ordinarily; the sublime, conceived of as a superior substitute for ordinariness, made it imperative for individuals to immerse themselves in dramatic landscapes, heroic journeys and aspire to artistic greatness. The sublime also readily degenerates into 'self-indulgent feelings of guilt' – as is the case with some variants of deconstructionism (*MGM*, p. 223). The focus here is on the failure of the sublime to offer more than a faint hope of moderate overcoming; the fragility and uncertainty of progress inflames an overwhelming sense of defeat that is as grandly romantic as it is pessimistic. The thinking is that 'all that is left us is the endless study of the determination of subjectivity by language'.

The thought that humans discern the truth by way of its uniquely educative effect – although problematic for human psychology and philosophy conceived of on the model of scientism – is not uncommon and receives expression in literature, biography autobiography and memoir. One such articulation of it is by the main character of a recent novel by Peter Pouncey, *Rules for Old Men Waiting*. He reflects:

> The fact is that we do learn from each other, especially those we admire or love. That is perhaps why we have schools. We can come, if we are blessed, to see things different, because we've been shown a better look. Captain Leslie was going to chase after young Tim Callum and throw the book at him, which is what army regulations and the law specified should be done. But then Private Alston sits next to him, and in a quiet tidy way shows him the whole matter can stop right here, and everyone better for it. And Leslie takes the view as his own, because it's better. And also perhaps because, quite apart from this particular judgment, there was a larger one: the fact is that Leslie knows Alston is a better man than he is, and he wants to be like him. (Pouncey 2005, pp. 198–9)

A better look just is a look that we recognize as better. The argument is circular but need not be vicious, in large part because we are historical beings. As individuals we frequently and repeatedly find ourselves in either Leslie's or Alston's position – in possession of a better vision or the recipient of a better vision – and it is in the context of this dialogue, within and amongst ourselves, that we find insurance against such circularity.

What is misleading about the quotation from *Rules for Old Men Waiting* is that it represents the adoption of a better look as smooth, quick and painless, whereas in reality progress is typically more arduous, painstakingly slow, hard-won, incremental and often imperceptible. It involves, as Murdoch describes it, 'a disciplined destruction of false images and false goods' (*MGM*, p. 320). Not everyone abandons their look as quickly as Leslie did or comprehends a new look as easily. This is because our looks serve deep psychological needs which makes the transition all the more difficult. Further, these better looks approach and attempt 'to express what is perfectly good, but extremely remote' (*MGM*, p. 320). It is for this reason perhaps that 'Kant's more "democratic" less ecstatic morality envisages a more modest continually renewed daily achievement under the concepts of reason and duty' (*MGM*, p. 320).

Humans recognize a better look by way of their desire to inhabit it. It follows that the search for wisdom or understanding is not just an intellectual exercise, but involves the whole person, transforming not only what is seen, but desire and behaviour as well. This makes sense if we recall that a look is appreciated as better relative to its educative force. A look is educative if it is capable of reorienting the individual: the situation looks different because the individual is differently placed with respect it. For example, it becomes impossible for Leslie, on learning of Alston's better look, innocently to act on his original plan. He might have chosen to act other than he did, but he would now need a justification for himself. Leslie's whole person is claimed by Alston's better look. It is the magnetism of Alston's better look that is the source of Leslie's energy for action – he knows what he has to do. Alston's look is better not only because it is more efficient, practical and honest but it is better in some absolute sense that is informed by Leslie's perception of Alston.

Leslie understands Alston's look as better because he recognizes his desire to *be* like Alston. Not in the sense of slavishly imitating him – although for many of us, this is part of the learning process – but in the sense of becoming more perfect as Leslie. In Alston, Leslie realizes that it is possible to be and do better, and that he has a sense of what it might look like: simple, tidy, thoughtful, considerate of others, discrete and with integrity. Leslie is attracted to the possibility for himself that he sees in Alston. A natural step in the direction of that possibility is for Leslie to accept and inhabit Alston's better look, at least in this particular instance. Leslie is guided by the love inspired by Alston to seek out what it represents for him, in an effort to become more perfect. Similarly, for readers of Plato, the idea of the form of the good, serves 'as active creative sources of energy in the world' (*MGM*, p. 223). It resists the absorption by the patterns of consciousness and works to transform them.

According to Murdoch, if a metaphysical theory can cause a reorientation of consciousness in the direction of greater truthfulness and goodness then it is equivalent to a religious sacrament. A religious sacrament is an act, ritual or ceremony that is an occasion of spiritual grace; the activity, ritual or ceremony derives its significance from what it imparts rather than from its own definition. It is symbolic of a psychic change that it is also a stimulus for.[11] A sacrament is a source of good or redirected energy and it is this good energy that saves us from ourselves, in particular the falsifying and self-serving habits and patterns of our own consciousness. If 'value is everywhere' then 'the whole of life is movement on a moral scale' (*MGM*, p. 56).

In summary, religious philosophies place human beings on the continuum between truth and falsity, reality and fantasy, good and evil. The human condition is characterized by the promise of truth, reality and goodness, our efforts to accomplish them, and the inevitable impossibility of the task. We are, as Murdoch writes, 'continuously striving and learning, discovering and discarding images' (*MGM*, p. 249). Plato and Kant understand that to be human is not to be given in a fixed relationship to goodness and truth but to be always in the process of becoming more or less good and more or less wise. This is because we find ourselves, as human beings, in the midst of working out what goodness and truth consist in. This working out 'concerns the continuous detail of human activity' and so it is not exclusively intellectual (*MGM*, p. 11). What we discover has the effect of checking or strengthening our desires, intensifying or diluting our faith in 'our ability to discover the truth', bolstering or undermining our confidence in the inner life (*MGM*, pp. 402, 183). For Plato and Kant at least, 'it involves the whole of man and attaches value to the most "concrete" of everyday preoccupations and acts'. To be human is to be taken up 'with the continual activity of our own minds and souls and with our own possibilities of being truthful and good' (*MGM*, pp. 249–50). Hence Murdoch concludes that for both Plato and Kant, 'education is moral education' or 'moral progress' (*MGM*, pp. 175, 177).

Religious philosophies have ambiguity as their final limit: it is impossible to determine, with absolute certainty, that what is taken to be 'real' or 'true' is an accurate reflection of the way things are. The omnipresence of an ultimate ambiguity does not prevent Plato and Kant from maintaining a 'religious certainty about the fundamental and ubiquitous reality of goodness: their real world is the moral world' – another reason for Murdoch's designation of them as 'religious philosophies' (*MGM*, p. 50). Their philosophies demonstrate 'a deep and certain moral insight' (*MGM*, p. 11). For example, Plato's metaphysical argument for the form of the good is 'a mythical religious vision' (*MGM*, p. 399). Murdoch writes that Plato 'knew that Good was not only real but supremely so . . . He knew that morality, an orientation between good and evil, was in a unique sense fundamental and ubiquitous in human life' (*MGM*, p. 402).[12] According to Murdoch, it is Plato's 'faith [loving belief]' in the reality of goodness that enables him to interpret its presence in the meanderings of practical, ordinary and everyday moral life (*MGM*, p. 393).

Murdoch acknowledges that although the philosophies of Plato and Kant are similar in emphasis – they start from a position of the omnipresence of value – there are significant differences between the two. They remain on different sides of the divide. Plato gathers 'value together in its purest form in the Idea (form) of the Good' and Kant gathers it together in 'the operation of practical reason' (*MGM*, p. 56). For Plato, the good is 'brought back to the world' through truthfulness and purified desire (love, Eros), whereas Kant 'brings value back to the world through conceptions of truth and justice incarnate in the recognition of duties' (*MGM*, p. 56). Murdoch argues that these differences are of 'theological' interest. Here she suggests that the differences between the philosophies of Plato and Kant are a matter of how one likes to picture *the details* and, as in the case of religion, individuals may find one 'theology' more psychologically powerful than the other.

Conclusion

Murdoch's philosophy of the 'third way' informs her philosophizing, literary style and hermeneutics of reading. It also falls within the tradition of philosophical romanticism. This is not surprising when one considers Murdoch's own designation of Plato and Kant as 'the great romantics': philosophers who understand the fictional status of their philosophies that comment on our human striving for the transcendent from a situation of finitude and contingency. Further, the philosophies of Plato and Kant uniquely sustain the following paradoxical tensions: imagination as a source of both delusion and imagination as a source of truth; all education as moral education; and the dual ideal of self-expression (artist) and self-denial (saint). These features lead to the account of philosophical romanticism that follows in the next chapter.

Chapter 3

Romanticism Reconsidered

Introduction

The romantic philosophical tradition has been enjoying a revival in recent years.[1] In this chapter, I provide an overview of this tradition as the framework for my consideration of Murdoch's philosophy. I explicate a set of definitive romantic ideas as the lens through which to read Murdoch's philosophy, focusing and organizing our interpretive gaze. As a preface to this overview, it is worthwhile restating that although philosophical romanticism informs my analysis of Murdoch's philosophy, it is not my principal research focus.[2] I aim to provide a partial and preliminary account of philosophical romanticism that is adequate for my purposes. I do not claim to provide a full analysis of the romantic philosophical tradition or to intervene in its scholarly debates. It is important to note at the outset, however, that there are a number of factors that make even a partial account of philosophical romanticism difficult.

First, the term 'romanticism' is used retrospectively to describe an historical period in Europe and America that varied according to geography and time.[3] Hence, Beiser speaks of early German romanticism as 'a very protean movement, passing through several phases and undergoing several transformations' (Beiser 2003, p. 44). This suggests that no one figure or group of figures is uniquely representative of romanticism. Romanticism is not a unified philosophy position, but a tradition of interrelated thinkers whose writings revolve around a set of abiding philosophical concerns.

Second, until recently, twentieth-century Anglo-American philosophers had not given serious consideration to romanticism, considering it a literary rather than philosophical movement. Further, the little that had been written tends to be highly critical. Romanticism is condemned for valorizing anti-rationalism: that which is in excess of reason, like intuition and passion, is considered fundamental to subjectivity and of most interest to it. The romantic individual is caught in a paradox of enquiring into those features of subjectivity that precisely resist the kind of rational enquiry that she feels compelled to conduct. Along similar lines, romanticism is censured for its unhealthy preoccupation with the self, as both artistic project – the creation and embodiment of a beautiful soul – and the transcendent, mysterious ground of that creative project. Romanticism is also criticized for compromising fundamental democratic commitments by encouraging the active differentiation of exemplary human beings on the basis of originality, sensitivity, nobility, spontaneity and beauty. Eldridge is right to observe that romanticism has had 'a bad press throughout much of the twentieth century' (Eldridge 2001, p. 1).

The third reason for why an overview of philosophical romanticism is so difficult concerns its literariness. Romantic philosophers typically write in forms – fragments, stories, dramas and poems – that do not lend themselves easily to philosophical analysis. Novalis, for example, mixed prose and verse in the poem *Hymns to the Night* and wrote fragments, as well as the novel *Henry of Ofterdingen*. Hölderlin wrote poetry, Schlegel wrote fragments and Schelling wrote the novel *Clara or, On Nature's Connection to the Spirit World*. The romantic reliance on the literary genre to convey and constitute philosophical meaning makes it difficult for academic philosophers – trained in the presentation, analysis and evaluation of explicit arguments – to engage profitably with romantic texts. Hermeneutical understanding of romantic thought necessitates an ability to read diverse literary genres, as each contributes to the formulation of thinking expressed. As Fiona Steinkamp writes in her Introduction to Schelling's *Clara*, 'its very structure reflects its content' (Schelling 2002, p. vii).

The genre of the novel stresses the sheer openendedness of human becoming and its determination by contingency. The genre of the fragment stresses the incompleteness of all finite knowing, and the promise of expressing this incompleteness. The genre of the poem combines openness with precision, association with reflection, and elusiveness with concentrated thought. All three genres represent philosophical thought as occurring in the context of the condition that makes for its possibility: namely, the unfolding life of the person as it involves temporality, a rich emotional life, memory, nostalgia, inspiration, nagging doubts and yearning. These genres also stress the polyphonic nature of human value: if the infinite is to be expressed in finite form then it is necessary that there be infinitely many possibilities for that expression.

In summary, romanticism does not represent an explicit philosophical position. It typically receives scant attention from philosophers and the attention that it does receive tends to be critical. Philosophers interested in elucidating romantic thought are frequently confounded by the literariness of the thought's expression and the view that literary expression is constitutive of thought itself. These difficulties aside, it is possible to make some generalizations and highlight defining characteristics of philosophical romanticism. My account of philosophical romanticism draws from a range of contemporary scholars (Richard Eldridge, Jane Kneller, Charles Larmore, Nikolas Kompridis, Robert Pippin and Martin Seel) but relies most heavily on Frederick C. Beiser's analysis of early German romanticism (c. 1797–1801).[4]

Beiser's work is prominent in my analysis for three reasons. First, he argues that the central ideas of early German romanticism 'were primarily ethical and political rather than critical or literary' (2003, p. 24).[5] Beiser's construal of the romantic project as ethical is important for my purposes because it establishes a clear link to Murdoch's philosophy. They share a common undertaking, namely to address the following questions: 'What is a good man like? How can we make ourselves morally better? *Can* we make ourselves morally better?' (*SG*, p. 52)

The second reason for my reliance on Beiser's scholarship is that he emphasizes and explicates the uniquely romantic commitment to paradoxical truth. In brief, philosophical romanticism defends freedom *and* necessity, religion and humanism, passivity and activity, and philosophy and poetry. Murdoch shares this commitment which is most noticeably present in her claim that virtue is absolutely pointless and supremely important (*SG*, p. 86). The centrality of paradox, for both the romantics and Murdoch's thought justifies her location within this philosophical tradition.

Finally, Beiser insists that romantic aestheticism be framed by its Platonist underpinnings (2003, p. 61). Early German romanticism is, he argues, the 'greatest revival of Platonism since the Renaissance' (Beiser 2003, p. 59).[6] Murdoch's later revival of Plato places her within the romantic tradition and makes early German romantic scholarship an appropriate hermeneutical context for her writings.

Platonic revivals

According to Beiser, the most relevant aspect of Plato's thought for early German romanticism is its objective or absolute idealism, making everything conform 'to the idea, the purpose, the *logos* of things' (Beiser 2003, p. 66).[7] Accordingly, reason is an intuitive as well as a discursive faculty (p. 62). It is ' "an intellectual power of seeing" which is indeed ecstatic' (p. 72). Reason operates perceptively, as well as procedurally, to discover features of a given world that, although real, are not available to the senses. There is a relationship of inextricable intimacy between these discernible features and the world as given, for to discover these features just *is* to see one's world anew. Everything within the world is altered and reorganized in light of discerning a new feature. Aesthetic reason is holistic in the sense that it involves a grasp of the whole, over and above knowledge of the parts. It perceives reality in light of a unifying, whole-making image, acting in her other *persona* as imagination. Features of a given world are equivalent to Platonic forms in that they incarnate the absolute in appearance or, alternatively, embody the infinite in the finite. They are perceived indirectly, by the 'eye' of reason, according to how they inform and shape direct sensorial experience.

As a perceptive power, reason is ultimately imperfect. This is because attempting to know the infinite, absolute or unconditioned – that which exceeds its limits – reason engages in a falsification by bringing the infinite, absolute or unconditioned within the compass of its representational powers. Reason cannot but render the infinite in exclusively finite terms, but to do so is to falsify the infinite, making it finite. All is not lost, however, because such a process entails a subtle shift in our understanding of the finite terms – they come to have a less literal and more metaphorical status. True wisdom combines 'hyper-rational mysticism' with tenacious 'scepticism' (Beiser 2003, p. 67). The romantics conclude that because humanity cannot do without the perceptive insights of reason, it is imperative for individuals passionately to exercise their reason in this manner. The inherent imperfection of reason and its inevitable falsification of that which it perceptually discovers necessitates that individuals be vigilant in their employment of it, constantly attending to the possibility of false totalities. Individuals in the exercise of reason must observe its limits in the integration of them into the enquiry. These limits are not overturned, transformed into limitations that must be overcome; rather they remain as constitutive guides that navigate the individual's quest for understanding.

The romantic revival of Plato's absolute idealism generates three ideas that are archetypal of philosophical romanticism and central to Murdoch's philosophy. The first is that individuals are always and inevitably becoming, they are constantly destroying old selves and creating new selves as they engage in ongoing renewal. Given that the rational perception of a feature of a given world entails seeing an entirely new world, what emerges is that with each newly discovered feature the individual acquires a new, richer and larger perspective that is able to reflect on deficits of past perspectives, and locates her differently within reality, allowing her to act in new ways. The individual is engaged in a continuous process of destruction and regeneration with respect to the self. But there is a paradox at the heart of becoming. A condition for the possibility of the self is the sequence of old selves that preceded it; and yet the identity of the new self as *new* is, in large part, constituted by a perspective on the old selves as inherently flawed – a perspective not available to it before.

A second archetypal romantic idea shared by Murdoch is that love is the privileged expression of reason in its relationship to the infinite. In this context, love describes an ethical and epistemological orientation, rather than a strictly psychological one. Love is a passionate, deferential attachment to an experience or, more accurately, an image that, although it eludes the individual's conceptual understanding, inspires her to 'speak to' her engagement with it as uniquely authoritative. It is in 'speaking to' the conceptually resistant and authoritative that the individual deepens her conceptual understanding while remaining within the limits of reason.

Platonic love, in this sense, resembles our experience of intimate romantic love. Falling in love with another is not based on a set of predetermined objective criteria that the beloved fulfils; individuals are frequently mystified by 'falling in love' and the individuals with whom they fall in love given the apparent lack of basis in 'fact'. Inspired by love, the lover seeks to answer to the particular authority of the beloved in how she speaks and behaves towards that other. Through this process the lover is transformed, often for the better although sometimes in a way that is more degraded, depending on the object of love. Individuals that experience falling in love will speak about 'finding their true self', 'becoming whole' and 'feeling truly energized' – these feelings are themselves part of the appeal that falling in love has for us, for they promise new possibilities for self-realization.

It should come as no surprise to discover, therefore, that the early German romantics were fascinated by the process of 'falling in' and 'out' of love as a 'starting-point' for thinking about reason's relationship to the transcendent (*SG*, p. 75). Murdoch agrees with romantics that 'falling in love' is a subspecies of Platonic love, but is much more sceptical about it as a potential site for philosophical analysis and insight. In her view, the cumulative effect of reason's repeated efforts 'to do justice' to the poignancy, uniqueness and profound significance of 'falling in love' has, perversely, resulted in a dominant cultural myth of romantic love. Too readily swayed by fears, desires, fantasies and cultural norms, individuals readily forget reason's falsifying imperfection, choosing to accept the redemptive narrative rather than the grace of redemption itself. Murdoch is concerned that an individual's ability really to 'fall in love' is compromised by our complacent refusal to question reason's totalizing inadequacy in this regard – a concern most evident in her novels. Love, like becoming, has a paradoxical status. Human love 'is the most important thing of all' but is 'normally too profoundly possessive and also too "mechanical" to be a place of vision' (*SG*, p. 75).

The third significant archetypal idea is irony or, in Murdoch's case, humility. Both enact a striving for truth and an acknowledged inability to attain it. Irony represents the romantic recognition that although truth is unattainable, it is nonetheless approachable and, as a consequence, a necessary object of aspiration and striving. To be ironical is to be intelligently detached from our critical and creative powers in an acknowledgement of their limits and a vigilant responsiveness to their excess. To quote Beiser, we do not want our powers to 'completely expend themselves in the heat of inspiration' (2003, p. 130). The romantic focus on irony is so much deeper than it initially appears. Rather than a mere stylistic or intellectual flourish, irony recalls absolute idealism. As humanity's cautionary angel, irony governs an individual's relationship to any and all disclosures of the world; it is a meta-imperative enacted in all practices of seeing, thinking and acting.

In Murdoch's view, irony does not go far enough because the ability to be ironical presents as a sophisticated accomplishment, turning attention back towards a glorified self. It risks becoming equivalent to reason, imagination, freedom and other substitutes by securing human redemption: for to be ironical is to be enlightened. Humility is formally similar to irony but without drawing attention to the self. Humble people are 'hard to picture' and 'least illuminating', Murdoch writes (*SG*, p. 53). It would be a mistake to believe that humble individuals are less visible because they have less robust selves due to the longsuffering subordination of their own interests, desires, passions and commitments to those of others. Humility is entirely compatible with a robust self. The significance of a humble individual is her deep and mature ability to deflect the right kind of attention from others towards the objects that she herself attends to and loves. She is educator, first and foremost.

Humility, more so than irony, implies that the engagement of distance with respect to our critical and creative powers is a necessarily moral as well as intellectual exercise. Such distancing is difficult because it involves a suspension of our *ethical* commitments as they inform our epistemic ones: it is to distance and genuinely hold in question our most profound commitment and values. Murdoch favours humility over irony because the ability successfully to enact an ironical posture in what one says requires a high degree of linguistic and semantic mastery, whereas humility is enacted behaviourally and is without measures of performative success.

These three ideas, typifying the romantic revival of Platonism carry over to my interpretation of Murdoch's subtle but significant modifications to romantic philosophy. 'Instances of the facts' that Murdoch wishes to resuscitate are 'that an unexamined life can be virtuous' and that 'love is a central concept in morals' (*SG*, pp. 1, 2). The significance of these two facts is *not* that they oppose reason, but that they illuminate reason in its orientation towards the infinite (good). Murdoch uses terms like 'consciousness' and 'imagination' in order to highlight reason as a perceptual and not just deliberative and practical faculty. Imagination is not intended to usurp the place of reason, but appears as reason in another persona. Murdoch analyses the implications of an imaginatively constituted world and self, focusing particularly on reason's perverse nature – its susceptibility to error – in the form of totalizing fantasies, consoling narratives, projection, narcissism and sado-masochism.

The three ideas that I have outlined in the context of a romantic revival of Platonic philosophy also resonate with Immanuel Kant – they are as much Kantian as they are Platonic. Hence, my outline of philosophical romanticism begins with the writings of Kant: I explain that although early German romanticism formulated itself as a rejoinder to Kant's critical philosophy, its resources were drawn from within Kant's philosophy, in particular *The Critique of Judgement*. I conclude that the apparent disjunction between Kant's critical philosophy and the ideas of early German romanticism is constitutive of a deeper underlying continuity. Whereas Kant examines the transcendental conditions for the possibility of both theoretical and practical reason, romanticism explores the transcendental conditions for the possibility of imaginative reason. Aesthetic appreciation and creation are seen as analogues for wisdom, freedom and self-realization, or *Bildung*, as the ultimate human achievements.

Kantian reverberations

Early German romanticism begins in the late eighteenth century, following Kant's 'humanization of the world'. Romanticism is a reaction to Kant's critical philosophy and its cultural legacies, in particular the development and dominance of science as epistemically paradigmatic.[8] Science conceives of nature as governed by laws and it aspires to a complete articulation of these laws. The problem occurs when science becomes epistemically paradigmatic, resulting in the 'theorizing away' of a morally and aesthetically illuminating engagement with the world. There is nothing in science that provides the individual with 'a sense of the *meaning* of nature' (Bowie 1990, p. 3; emphasis added). A conception of experience modelled on science impoverishes 'our world' by depleting it of feeling, meaning and significance. Kant's critical philosophy initiated a conception of value as 'reduced or denuded', leaving no alternative but to locate authority of ethical and aesthetic value in the self (Lockbridge 1989, p. 3). This effect was to separate empirical (natural) and normative (aesthetic and ethical) worlds, and leave human beings to straddle them precariously.

Kant acknowledges this impasse in the Introduction to the *Critique of Judgement*. He had created an irreparable gulf between phenomenal and noumenal reality by defining noumenal reality as something which could not be known – except as phenomenally determined by time, space and the categories – and could only be expressed through an individual's autonomous action. The impasse was two-pronged. Although Kant had ascertained minimal criteria for objectivity within subjective experience, still he could not account for the successful discovery of empirical laws and classifications. Kant had developed an account of human freedom and agency, but could not explain how individuals were able to recognize themselves as free and how they knew whether, and when, the world was suitable for autonomous action. In an effort to bridge 'the external world of nature and the internal world of self-consciousness', Kant became concerned with aesthetic judgement and artistic creation (Bowie 1990, p. 2).

Kant analyses the aesthetic as a mediating faculty: mediating between necessity and freedom; between the noumenal and the phenomenal; between the practical and the theoretical; and between the sensuous and the rational. He names it 'the faculty of judgement', arguing that it uniquely provides individuals with an oblique but powerful awareness of their own freedom ('Analytic of the Sublime') and of the world as compatible both with their empirical understanding ('The Critique of Teleological Judgement') and freedom ('Analytic of the Beautiful'). In aesthetic judgement, intimations of the supersensible substrate of nature (beauty) and humanity (sublimity) are received. In the case of beauty, the imagination and understanding spontaneously harmonize around a given representation, and a feeling of disinterested pleasure is produced. The individual experiences the representation as having an inherent (non-imposed) and authoritative form. In the case of sublimity, nature exceeds the representative powers of the imagination. The feeling of exhilaration that the sublime produces testifies to our freedom.

Kant aptly describes the phenomenological character of this union between the noumenal and phenomenal in aesthetic experience but, importantly, does not provide an explanation. His reluctance derives from a desire to do justice to the aesthetic while adhering to his earlier philosophy and its restriction of knowledge to appearances. Kant is happy to leave open the question of why, in aesthetic experience, the union between the noumenal and the phenomenal occurs. He surmises that aesthetic experience inclines us to believe that it is *as if* God existed and that he were an artist, having created nature according to artistic principles. Like Kant, Murdoch accepts the mysteriousness of the union, but goes much further, arguing that it is only in relation to the union *as mysterious* that the grace of genuine human redemption is possible. Murdoch's view is that it is precisely Kant's openness to the essential ambiguity of the union that differentiates him from romanticism and distinguishes him as one of 'the great romantics' (*SG*, p. 85).

Kant's *Critique of Judgement* had a negative rather than positive significance for the early German romantics (Beiser 2003, p. 79). They found themselves indebted to the *Critique of Judgement* but also used it to cast severe judgement on Kant's critical philosophy.[9] In their view, Kant's account of subjectivity was inadequate and did not provide the necessary principle for 'grounding our place in the world' (Beiser 2003, p. 27). The romantics strove for an account of subjectivity that redressed the imbalances of Kant's earlier account. They expanded their account of subjectivity to go beyond the subject's ability to understand nature according to law-governed regularities or to act in accordance with universalizable duties. They included the subject's ability to appreciate and create beauty; the subject's ability to be inspired by natural forces; and the subject's ability to exemplify our humanity for others. The romantics perceived Kant's nascent aesthetic philosophy as a model for how they could overcome the legacy of his critical philosophy. It is with aesthetic judgement that Kant returns to humanity what he had previously denied it, namely replenishing the values of the world. Although focused on the aesthetic experience, romanticism did not consider it as an end, for its significance was primarily ethical and political.

Beiser concludes that romanticism is not a 'doctrine of political indifference or escapism' (2003, p. 41). Instead, it makes beauty 'the very touchstone, sign, or criterion of moral and political value' (p. 41). Individuals romanticize the world in order to become beautiful (moral) souls and (political) communities (p. 8). The 'will to value', as Beiser aptly describes it, is the overriding ethical imperative of the romantic enterprise (p. 22). It is an imperative committed to pluralism, because it assumes that there are a myriad of ways, albeit finite, to express absolute value (p. 180); it is an imperative committed to irony because all modes by which absolute value is expressed are finite. The 'will to value' is made possible by the model of subjectivity and experience nascent in Kant's aesthetics. Kant's category of the aesthetic provides a beacon of hope for the early German romantics, promising a meaningful reality as the basis for the reunification of self and community (Rush 2006, p. 178). It introduces a much 'broader notion of experience' (Goodman 1990, p. 22).

Bolstered by their new faith, the romantics set about revitalizing humanity's experiential relationship to the world through an aesthetic reform of human experience (Bowie 1990, p. 3). The magical mystery of the world was to be recovered through the power of contemplation. Contemplation educates our vision to appreciate the infinite in its transfiguration of the finite, the sacred in its transfiguration of the profane, and the absolute in its transfiguration of the contingent. Aesthetic reason brings 'into the phenomenal (sensible) world what Kant had treated as noumenal (supersensible) and non-empirical, while keeping the distinction between them intact' (Goodman 1990, p. 29). Those features of reality that exceed human comprehension are incarnated in, and made visible by, phenomenal experience. Simultaneously experiential and experientially transgressive, the aesthetic imagines ideas of reason – heaven, hell, eternity, hope and love, for example – by giving them symbolic expression. A poetics of carnality is born.

In the aesthetic, the meaning conveyed is inextricable from the medium used to communicate that meaning. They are reciprocally reliant on one another. J.M. Bernstein describes this as 'an authentic binding of meaning and matter', definitive of aesthetic reason (2006, p. 145). Aesthetic reason establishes a relationship between freedom and nature that is simultaneously necessary and contingent. An individual finds an image from literature or history compelling when that image exemplifies and teaches something about human freedom (or dignity, love, grace or courage, for example). The individual feels that human freedom has been uniquely realized in relationship to a particular set of contingent events (Bernstein 2006, p. 166). Thus, to consider what freedom means is to think about the materiality of its meaning (p. 145, 166). Like Murdoch, Bernstein is concerned to highlight that the understanding made possible by this precarious relationship between meaning (necessity) and materiality (contingency) is vulnerable to 'denial, collapse, and loss' (p. 166). It is fragile.

Romanticism accepts the Kantian insight that experience originates in humanity, but believes that aesthetic experience takes individuals out of themselves and joins them with the absolute. Aesthetic experience 'is the criterion, instrument and medium for awareness of ultimate reality or the absolute' (Beiser 2003, p. 74). The absolute is 'a goal we can approach but never completely attain', and so our relationship to it is characterized by 'eternal *striving* and *longing*' (p. 21). Individuals aspire to know absolute reality absolutely, but only ever do so imperfectly and incompletely: we falsify reality in the act of grasping it because reality, by definition, resists articulation in language. Humanity finds itself located in the between – between the infinite and finite, absolute and contingent, fate and freedom – hence, as Schlegel famously comments, 'becoming' is the defining feature of the romantic subject (Beiser 2003, p. 17).[10] At best, reality 'shows' itself as a magnetic field of influence on language, enabling a re-inscription of reason as perceptual and limited.

This overview provides the background necessary for interpreting romantic formulations of such ideas as love, art, irony, freedom, agency and *Bildung*. In the next section, I briefly summarize each of these concepts, explaining how they fit within the broader romantic perspective.

Romantic resolve

The question of whether or not the 'magnetism' of reality is genuine remains unresolved. It is impossible for us to know with certainty that what reason 'sees' is not a projection of human psychology. Our only compass for navigating the inherent ambiguity of aesthetic experience is love (reason's other persona). In an experience of love, reality 'comes alive' of its own accord and effects a change in the consciousness of the lover. It is an occasion, perhaps long-term, of being awed, inspired and overwhelmed by an individual, idea, image or object. To be claimed in love is to be drawn to that item of the world as expressing the *totality* of the world. The beloved embodies a totality that the lover recognizes but does not quite comprehend. The lover seeks to answer to the claim of the beloved as she seeks to discover what that claim consists of. She transforms old conceptual understandings in an effort to respond appropriately to the beloved's claim on her. The lover is actively open, intelligently seeking and enlisting available conceptual resources, in an effort to move towards and unify with the beloved.

Inspired by love, the lover allows herself to be determined by that which constitutes the authority of the beloved in an effort to develop 'a respectful determinedness' of the beloved (Seel 2006, p. 94). This 'respectful determinedness' is neither fully comprehensive nor conducted in solipsistic isolation. 'Respectful determinedness' involves the wish 'to determine *in* concert' with the other, in the recognition of the inherent openness and vulnerability of such an exercise. If beauty is 'freedom in appearance' then the romantic subject aspires not only to appreciate beauty, but realize such a freedom in the beauty of her own person (Beiser 2003, p. 99–100).

The early German romantics considered artistic creativity to be the consummate subjective expression of the absolute. According to Beiser, the romantics considered 'the creativity of the artist, philosopher, or saint' as the 'highest degree of organization and development of the divine force'. He writes that 'what the artist created is what the divine created through him, so that his work was nothing less than a revelation of the divine' (Beiser 2003, p. 143). Art existed as the 'self-production of the absolute' (p. 75). Unlike classical art, however, romantic art strove to reflect its own paradoxical status, drawing attention to its artificiality and truthfulness.

In order to do this, artists and philosophers had to reflect the incompleteness of their aspirations in the self-contained completeness of their achievements. The philosophical fragment was ideal for this because it is simultaneously a complete whole and an incomplete part, symbolizing the gap between a philosopher's aspirations and achievement. Romantics wanted to reveal within the parameters of an artistic creation the artist's own attitude towards the epistemic status of that creation. The artistic creation presented a perspective on the world and a respective distancing from it. For example, the artist would express reality in the recognition that any such expression is necessarily partial and perspectival (Rush 2006, p. 180). The romantics used literary form, in particular irony, to reflect the epistemic status of their reflection.

Irony is a complex concept for the romantics. On a basic level, it 'demands standing above all one's beliefs and creations through relentless self-criticism' (Beiser 2003, p. 51). But this self-criticism takes a particular form in the context of romanticism, commenting on the relationship between the conditioned (finite) and the unconditioned (infinite). The ironist recognizes that any conditioned expression of the unconditioned is not definitive and yet that, as human beings, we uniquely approach the unconditioned by striving to express it. As Beiser writes of Schlegel, 'only if we presuppose and strive toward the ideal of a complete communication will we achieve a deeper perspective, a richer concept, and a clearer statement of truth' (Beiser 2003, p. 130). Romantic irony is *not* a sceptical position: its purpose is 'to goad our striving, to intensify our efforts, so we approach closer to the ideal of a complete system' (p. 34). It is a form of commitment, as Fred Rush states: 'Irony is just what it *is* to be a committed, finite being. One commits in the face of the knowledge that any finite mode of life cannot exhaust the absolute, one does not fail to commit because of it' (Rush 2006, p. 187). The ironical stance reveals the author's own extraordinary effort 'to overcome the necessary limitations of human accomplishments by the sovereignty of the human spirit which rises above the contingencies of its own creations and ironically contrasts the absolute idea with the frailty of its symbolic representation' (Beiser 2003, p. 130). The romantic aim was to embody the unknowability of reality in the depiction of its reverberations in our unison with it.

Inherent in romantic irony is a distinctive conception of human freedom. The romantics reject both Kant's conception of freedom as original causality and Johann Gottlieb Fichte's existentialist conception of freedom as self-positing. Romanticism rejects these conceptions because they reify the noumenal–phenomenal divide. Instead, the romantic thinkers conceive of freedom as reconciliation to necessity. A self is free when she is reconciled to the necessity of her own nature and acts accordingly (Beiser 2003, p. 151). As a finite part of nature, the self is less than free, but as an infinite self, in its unity with nature, the self can be free. Here philosophical romanticism walks a middle line between a heroic conception of freedom (existentialist and Kantian – the 'I' as all-determining) and conceiving of freedom as devastated by necessity (Stoic and post-structuralism – the necessity of surrender). For the romantics, freedom 'arises from sharing or participating in divine necessity, in seeing that in all my actions the divine acts through me' (Beiser 2003, p. 151).[11]

If philosophical romanticism has a distinctive conception of freedom, then it also has a distinctive conception of agency. It sees agency 'as a matter of what we let ourselves be affected by rather than a matter of exercising control over what we encounter' (Kompridis 2006, p. 2). It gives a certain kind of prominence to 'the state of being determined that lies at the heart of human determining' (Seel 2006, p. 81). There is an obvious sense in which human beings are determined by their embodiment, sexuality, age, race, ethnicity, culture and history; and sometimes it is possible for individuals to make decisions about which of these they would like to be more prominent. This sense of determination and related questions dominates contemporary discourses in philosophy, cultural studies, politics and education. But there is also a positive sense to 'being determined' that reflects our affinities with the world and what we consider to make legitimate claims on us. As Pippin argues, 'our sense of self is essentially a sense of values we can't give up in the face of demands of others' (Pippin 2006, p. 121).

Not every value is worth committing to, but even the recognition of a value allows an individual to moderate her commitments. Only when an individual lets herself be moved by her affinities can she begin to reconcile them with what she considers valuable and, in the process, begin to determine what kind of life she might actually want to live. The process is double-sided: on one side an individual is free so long as her motivations are a genuine reflection of her values; on the other, an individual is free only if she considers her values worth pursuing. It is only when both elements are in place that the individual will experience her decisions as independent and binding. The process is 'open-ended', experimental and provisional at best. It requires a willingness to 'try on' different values and to 'allow within one's sense of determination a sense of the indeterminate' (Seel 2006, p. 92).

Inherent in this conception of freedom is the process of becoming. This process involves discovery and invention – it is not to have propositional knowledge of a pre-existing essence, but neither is it blind self-creation – it involves being true to one's self, when what one's self is remains always and inevitably open. Who we are becoming is 'always something provisional and hypothetical, a matter of dispositions with uncertain realizations and commitment of uncertain strengths' (Pippin 2006, p. 134). According to Pippin, it involves the attempt to 'retrieve what really happened as one's own, or to recover who one "really" was. It is the attempt to avoid being trapped in some wish-fulfilment fantasy or in yet another, merely successive provisional point of view. And it is the attempt to avoid being merely subject to the interpretive will of another' (p. 115). Even this language is somewhat misleading, because it suggests that becoming oneself is something that an individual pursues directly and independently, whereas in reality it is not so straightforward. This is one reason that *Bildung*, the fullest development of an individual's powers, is of such importance for philosophical romanticism.

In the romantic view, life should be viewed as 'one long learning experience in which everyone participated' (Beiser 2003, p. 98). The more developed an individual's creative powers, the more enhanced her perception of 'the beauty of the world' and the greater her embodiment of the absolute. Education redeems humanity. Art is the chief instrument and culmination of this redemptive education, in part because it educates reason in her other *persona* as imagination – 'it was also essential *to inspire* the people, to touch their hearts and to arouse their imaginations' – and in part because the artist is viewed as 'as the very paragon of humanity' (Beiser 2003, pp. 94, 93). Art educates our sensibilities by teaching us how to perceive beauty (p. 94). It awakens the sensibilities of its audience to the potential omnipresence of beauty. Romantic *Bildung* also entails the cultivation of love where love is conceived as the ability to respond to what is recognizable but indeterminable. It inspires individuals to think, act and develop in accordance with principles of reality that they can sense but not determine.

Art sensitizes us to the beauty within ourselves, directing attention to our 'inner depths' and 'hidden resources' (Beiser 2003, p. 101). Individuals perceive their souls/selves as a work of art, striving to express infinite reality in all our appearances (gesture, speech, behaviour, activity). *Bildung* refers to this project of self-creation and perfection. A soul becomes more beautiful with an individual's expanding freedom; reason, affect and sensibility are increasingly integrated. A beautiful soul is reflected in the grace of an individual's demeanour, mirrored by others' aesthetic and ethical witness. Gracefulness occurs in the context of relation and, although essentially spontaneous, it is the result of sustained effort and discipline. The individual answers to necessity (the particular constraints of her lived situatedness) and to her freedom (the ability to transcend those constraints through a dignified and 'knowing' engagement with them).

Committed to its educational ideal, philosophical romanticism refrains from being programmatic. *Programmatic* educational reform is an oxymoron because it is contrary to the spirit of *Bildung*. Any programmatic reform will stifle crucially new opportunities for becoming – on the part of both teacher and student – because it deprives individuals of the opportunity to take responsibility for *who* they want to become. To put it another way, programmatic education encourages teachers and students to act either from duty (the educational practices that are instituted) or inclination (to react against those institutional practices) but in neither case do they act from love. Love is foundational for education *not* because it mediates between teacher and student (although this is part of the story), but because it allows both teachers and students to discern their values, modify those values in light of what they discover to be worthwhile, and to develop determinations of the world in accordance with those values.

Chapter 4

Resistance and Reconciliation

Murdoch's 'untimely' defence of value, imagination, beauty and art would have led to her being classified as a romantic had she not been so explicit in her criticisms of the movement. Close examination of her criticisms of romanticism reveals her underlying ambivalence and a somewhat more reconciled relationship to philosophical romanticism. Murdoch aspires to be associated with the classical Greeks, and Plato in particular – she represents herself as fighting under Plato's banner and as offering a footnote to the classical Greek tradition (*SG*, pp. 78, 45). Part of her reason for wanting this affiliation is that the classical Greeks seem 'incapable of romanticism and *a fortiori* of sentimentality; they also, a related point, seem devoid of masochism' (*MGM*, p. 499). Classical Greek thinking is invulnerable to such romantic perversions as self-indulgent sentiment, unrealistic self-aggrandizement and self-interested suffering because it predates the distinctively aesthetic standpoint established in the mid eighteenth century and it remains focused on a transcendent reality and not the self – to look at the self is to be so 'dazzled' by it that one cannot see anything else (*SG*, p. 31).[1] The classical Greek understood 'the ultimate state of man's homelessness' and the later attempt to recover their 'radical vision' failed in light of 'a kind of romantic heroism' (*MGM*, p. 76).

Romanticism failed in its recovery of classical Greek thought because it enlisted specifically Kantian aesthetic categories (beauty, sublimity and genius) in re-articulating a Platonic conception of reality. The concepts are used to convey the idea that reality exceeds our epistemic capabilities; enlightenment involves the cognitive, affective and imaginative faculties and ultimately consists in the betterment of the individual (the creation of a beautiful soul); and experience presents us with occasions when an individual's perspective is either harmonious (beauty) or discordant with reality (sublimity). Murdoch endorses these ideas and shares the romantic aspiration to revitalize them in a contemporary form. She is critical of the Kantian aesthetic categories, however, because they induce both a misconstrual of the limit of consciousness, as the purposelessly mechanistic, and self-identification with our freedom to create ourselves through choice and action. This error is problematic because it effectively unmoors the self from reality, inviting exaggerated ideas of human freedom (existentialism) or determinism (post-structuralism). The realization of either one's freedom or deterministic nature is a pseudo-solution that masquerades as being 'in good faith'. Murdoch concludes that although well-intentioned, romanticism ends up indulging our fascination with the importance of the self and its suffering.

Murdoch uses the term 'romanticism' as a rough and not technical label (*SG*, p. 84). Her sense of romantics as individualistic, self-indulgent, sentimental and exalted, reflects the stereotypical and not the recent scholarly view.[2] She describes it as a 'conviction of personal salvation' that in turn saves us 'from real pessimism' (*SG*, p. 50). She equates romanticism with mediocre art, which by romanticizing reality – despair, sin, death, nothingness – makes the intolerable tolerable. Murdoch works against such an overly romanticized and overly optimistic conception of the subject. She highlights the need for greater ambivalence about our romanticizing of the world: on the one hand it is absolutely necessary and inevitable, and yet, on the other hand, it is susceptible to our egoistic desire for consolation, reassurance and affirmation. She demands increased pessimism about the ability of individuals ever to truthfully 'romanticize the world'.

By locating Murdoch within the romantic philosophical tradition, I do *not* imply that she falls prey to her own criticisms. Her philosophy aims to do justice to 'ordinary' individuals without lapsing into a sentimentalizing fiction of the ordinary as uncontrived, naïve, simple and true – all of which is far from ordinary.[3] Murdoch is not replacing 'the artistic' with 'the ordinary' so as to deify it and protect it from contestation and analysis in terms of class, race, gender and power.[4] My purpose is to establish Murdoch's philosophy within a tradition of philosophical romanticism that is immune from her own criticisms. Murdoch's classification of Plato as a great romantic demonstrates her awareness of this tradition and her willingness to be identified with it.[5]

Murdoch's classification of Plato as a 'great romantic' acknowledges that any resuscitation of his thought that occurs after the romantic movement of the late 1700s, is inevitably located within a romantic tradition.[6] Given that early German romanticism revived Platonic studies, Murdoch's appeal to Plato in her chastisement of contemporary romanticism, inadvertently aligns her with that tradition.[7] Murdoch argues that unlike such great romantics as Plato and Kant, romanticism in general succumbs to the self-consoling, self-aggrandizing, egoistic fantasy mechanism, evidenced by the emergence of such literal-minded imperatives as a self-directed appreciation of nature and the transformation of one's life into a work of art

(*SG*, p. 85). Murdoch addresses romanticism's egoism, allowing the original romantic or religious impulse of Plato's and Kant's philosophies to emerge in revised form.

My position is that philosophical romanticism is perhaps more consonant with the Platonic tradition than Murdoch allows. She acknowledges this when she admits that she is not speaking 'of the great romantic artists and thinkers at their best, but of the general beaten track which leads from Kant to the popular philosophies of the present day' (*SG*, p. 82).

Murdoch's resistance to romanticism

Murdoch is not recognized as a philosopher of the romantic tradition for two reasons. She does not identify herself as a romantic philosopher, rather she refers to herself as 'a neo-Christian, Buddhist, Christian, or Christian fellow traveller' (*MGM*, p. 419). She uses religious language and imagery, conceiving her philosophy in terms of salvation, sacrament, pilgrimage, grace and redemption, for example; she is interested in the power of the demonic and the role of demonic individuals in our lives. Conradi argues that 'The broad movement of her thought is from an uneasy flirtation with existentialism towards a more religious picture which shares much with Buddhism'[8] (Conradi 2001, p. xiv). Second, Murdoch represents her own philosophy as diametrically opposed to romanticism. She accuses romanticism of self-indulgence; of putting 'too great a value upon sincerity and immediacy' (*EM*, p. 237); having an 'intellectual and unsuspicious' view of art (*EM*, p. 247); taking 'refuge in sublime emotions' (*EM*, p. 368); forcing 'a self-directed enjoyment of nature' (*EM*, p. 369); and making 'something of a cult of suffering' (*EM*, p. 132).

Murdoch is not as critical of, and removed from, romanticism, as she first appears. She thinks that the romantic and religious odysseys are analogous, for both view humanity as capable of being redeemed, or made better, either by reference to a higher order and purpose, as in the case of traditional religion, or by reference to a higher faculty, as in the case of romanticism. Murdoch argues that romanticism is as mistaken as traditional religion for presuming to know – and with that knowledge secure the existence of – that which saves humanity from ignominy and meaningless: namely, reason in the persona of imagination and love. Humans are subject to nature but ultimately superior to it; natural and artistic beauty expresses this superiority and inspires its realization in the soul. In accepting the foundational premise of religion and romanticism, that it is possible for humans to be redeemed and made better, Murdoch categorically rejects the possibility that humans can know what this redemption consists in. She favours the language of religion over romanticism because it alludes to a transcendent reality, whereas romanticism makes it seem too much like a matter of the self. Murdoch favours the experiences described by romanticism because encounters with art and nature are – being more secular than religious rites, sacraments and rituals – more familiar and approachable.

Murdoch attributes the romantic misapprehension of these experiences and their status as being 'objectively redemptive', to its derivation in Kant's austere puritan philosophy and his concession to experiences of respect, beauty and sublimity: only these experience trigger 'a kind of allowable, rather painful, thrill which is a by-product of our status as dignified rational beings' (*SG*, p. 82). On these occasions an individual feels herself to be at the limit of consciousness or, in Murdoch's language, at 'the barrier' (*MGM*, p. 267). For example, sublimity – 'the spectacle of huge and appalling things' – exhilarates in a 'way which is less than excellent ... [it] is nothing more than a form of romantic self-assertion' (*SG*, p. 73). Although subsidiary to Kant's overall critical project, the experiences of respect, beauty and sublimity attain pre-eminence in romanticism – to negative effect. Murdoch objects, not to the categories of beauty, sublimity and respect – as demonstrated by their pre-eminence in her philosophical writings – but to Kant's phenomenological analysis of them as carried over by the romantics. The concept of the sublime is a perfect example.

The concept of the sublime is a central pillar of Murdoch's philosophy (see Chapter 5). She accepts that individuals have experiences in which they encounter a limit to consciousness, and that these experiences crucially motivate us to become better-realized ethical individuals. She objects to Kant's particular construal of the limit and the conception of moral improvement that it entails. Murdoch is not of the view that nature, in its ability to resist, dwarf and devastate the products of human imagination, is constitutive of a representative limit; or that individuals are exhilarated by the discovery that the power of reason (freedom), in the form of purposefulness, supersedes that of nature. On this view, nature and art become symbolic externalization of humanity's inner originality, majesty and beauty. Such a view is problematic, according to Murdoch, because instead of confronting reality (the limit of consciousness) we are returned to the self in its poignant suffering dignity. Murdoch refers to this as 'a taming and beautifying of the idea of death, a cult of pseudo-death and pseudo-transience' (*SG*, p. 82).

People don't feel charm or exhilaration, even of a painful kind, when they truly encounter the formlessness of reality, death, unless that is they meet it with the assurance of an alternative reality – as in the case of religious salvation or the romantic appropriation of Kantian reason/ freedom. On Murdoch's view, the romantics are committing a version of Kant's 'fallacy of pure reason': reifying an idea of reason as if it were an independent and superior power to which we are required to submit. They neglect to appreciate that the idea of reason/freedom is not absolute, but the product of our own activity (Beiser 2003, p. 179). Romanticism is a form of metaphysical dogmatism, masquerading as critique; it is perverse and, as we know from Freud, perversion is an inextricable feature of the psyche.

In romanticism, the ideas of death and chance are idealized into a meaningful or necessary suffering. Suffering is the image of our 'tortured freedom' which is the result of our existence as rational individuals. To be romantic is to take refuge in the exaltation of this suffering freedom (*SG*, p. 83). The romantics replace death with suffering and combine it with 'a kind of (quasi-sexual) excitement' (*MGM*, p. 132). This vision of romanticism is 'more ordinary, more relaxed and more pleasure-seeking' than it first appears (*MGM*, p. 141). The romantics eclipse death and chance (two names for nothingness) by shifting attention away from the insufferable unknowability of reality to the subject's creative powers to represent and realize her freedom in relationship to the unknown. Romanticism leads us back to the 'angel-self', via individual suffering. Murdoch writes: 'How abject we are, and yet our consciousness is of infinite value' (*SG*, pp. 83, 82).

It is noteworthy that Murdoch does *not* criticize romanticism from the perspective of an alternative metaphysical theory. Her goal is not to replace one theoretically derived conception of reality with another, for she objects to the assumption upon which such a process is premised, namely that reality can in fact be theoretically derived. Instead, she uses her understanding of the human psyche (acknowledged by her as imperfect) to diagnose romanticism's theory of reality. She is suspicious of the theory because it returns attention back to the self; it presents the self as vindicated by its own creative freedom; and it encourages emotions of exaltation, excitement and thrill. These features evidence the fantasy mechanism of the ego, in particular, its desire to confront death without ever really having to do so – hence her criticism that romanticism replaces death with suffering. As a price of egoistic wish-fulfilment, romanticism is a falsifying theory. Murdoch's disposal of romanticism is not meant to imply that she has, therefore, the correct theory. It is not meant to imply anything other than that she has good reason to mistrust it.

Murdoch's other, related, reason for mistrusting romanticism is its elitism. Romantics – and here she includes almost every philosopher except Plato – are elitist in their relegation of redemptive possibility to the preserve of a very select few (geniuses, artists and beautiful souls). Theoretically romanticism deifies the artistic creation at the expense of other forms of human activity and expression. Heidegger, for example, privileges poeticized philosophy above all other forms of thinking, arguing that it is the most profound thought to which all individuals should aspire. Derrida is guilty because he differentiates individuals who are aware of how language codifies their subjectivity from the masses who are not. In all cases, awareness of consciousness *as consciousness* – an ability to touch the barrier – is limited to a select 'aesthetically, intellectually, enlightened few' (*MGM*, p. 267). Most of us are sunk in the 'deep ocean' of ordinary consciousness and only the enlightened elite that rise up 'into the sunshine while still belonging to the sea. (Like dolphins perhaps)' (*MGM*, p. 267).

Murdoch takes issue with this elitism because it results in a lack of accountability by the artist or philosopher-poet to ordinary language and individuals. If the artist or poetic philosopher perceives of himself as able to transcend consciousness, then he does not need to explain himself to others in order to be understood by them. He does not have to provide 'careful sober lucidity' or 'clarified reflections', if he possesses the enlightened and original vision that others are unlikely to understand (*MGM*, p. 267). Such a lack of accountability goes hand in hand with a profound contempt for ordinary consciousness and individuals. Romanticism promotes a culture of condescension towards most individuals: individuals who are neither geniuses, artists, poets nor intellectuals; individuals who do not enjoy spectacles of nature or have a fetish for language; and individuals who do not appear to live their lives as artistic projects. The romantics make the mistake of thinking that their conception of the transcendent is a model for how everyone *should* conceive it – they misapprehend their view as a categorical imperative.

Murdoch acknowledges that this temptation is particularly difficult for consciousness to resist for two reasons. First, it dissolves the inherent ambiguity of life in favour of the self and, second, there is some truth to the idea. For there are indeed exceptional individuals who 'gaze upon uncategorized manifolds and create new meanings, discover fresh categories, reinvent language' (*MGM*, p. 267). Even noting these difficulties, Murdoch is not dissuaded from contesting the elitism of romanticism. She argues that while it is true that consciousness involves the production of pictures, and some individuals have marginally more control over this activity than others, nevertheless these pictures – even the controlled ones – must be 'explained, used, related to human life, surrounded by clear plain language' (*MGM*, p. 267). These pictures should be explained because 'we all, not only can but *have* to, experience and deal with transcendent reality, the resistant otherness of other persons, other things, history, the natural world, the cosmos, and this involves perpetual effort. We are amazing creatures, no wonder Sophocles calls us *deinos*' (*MGM*, p. 268). Romanticism fails to recognize that *everyone*, and not just the genius artist and thinker, makes an effort to integrate their experiences of transcendent reality into life.

Romantic elitism derives in part from its egoism. Motivated by a desire to secure the importance of humanity against a meaningless reality, it locates the objective ground of humanity's importance in our appreciation and creation of beauty. Although it does not restrict this ability to the creative arts, nonetheless it has the effect of conferring paramount importance upon the creative artists. The creative artists are paragons of the kind of individuals that we aspire to become, for they have a demonstrably more refined sensibility. The problem with this view, according to Murdoch, is that it obfuscates the true nature of the effort to become better, as it precludes most individuals from participating in this effort. The effort to become better is not a matter of refining one's sensibilities, but rather of engaging in moral discipline. Becoming better involves moral effort, curbing the ego, reining in our fantasies, and accepting that we are far less important than we would like to believe. There are a number of noteworthy features of moral effort. First, it is something that, to different degrees, all individuals engage in nearly all of the time – this is part of Murdoch's meaning when she refers to human beings as moral conscripts. Second, moral effort is not requisite upon having a specialized faculty or expertise; moral effort is difficult, unpredictable, and is not even guaranteed by practice. Third, moral effort is personal and historical: it is something that individuals need to do for themselves and it changes over time.

If the romantics fail to appreciate the moral effort involved in becoming better, it is because they assume that they already know the objective ground of human importance (i.e. the romantics conceive of themselves as valuing what is true). It is Murdoch's refusal to locate human importance in any objective ground that enables her to appreciate that humans accept as true whatever they consider to be valuable. Individuals do not seek the truth so as to be inspired to desire it; rather they seek the truth so as to have the right desires. On Murdoch's view, individuals inextricably value certain activities, individuals and ideas over others. These values determine how we experience the world or, more accurately, what world we experience – what we accept as true. It is internal to the nature of valuing that individuals want to value what is most truly valuable: we want to love what is truly lovable; admire what is truly admirable and respect what is worthy of respect. Individuals do not wish to be deluded about what they find valuable.

If consciousness pictures reality according to what it values over all else, then an individual's endeavour to seek the most truthful values is not unique either to the genius artist or philosopher-poet. Instead, we are all making these peering efforts of attention most, if not all, of the time. As Murdoch says, we only need go 'as far as the category of the existing individual which Kierkegaard asserted against Hegel' (*MGM*, p. 268). It is to emphasize the universal and moral character of our becoming humanly better that Murdoch heralds her opposition to the mistaken dogmas of both the Enlightenment (reason) and romanticism (art) in the title of her early work *The Sovereignty of Good*. Neither reason nor art can be sovereign over the good, because to talk about reasoning is to talk about better and worse forms of it; and to talk about art is to talk about better and worse forms of it also. Only the good 'is the trial of itself and needs no other touch' (*SG*, p. 98).

Murdoch's resistance to existentialism

In *Metaphysics as a Guide to Morals* Murdoch responds to what she identifies as the Western philosophical tradition's *romantic break* with Plato's theory of truth, replacing it with a conception of value as a function of will (*SG*, p. 80). The Western philosophical tradition has released the individual 'into an open space wherein to *construct* his morality' (*MGM*, p. 40).[9] This is at the heart of the problem, for Murdoch, because if all values are chosen then the possibility of discovering true values is theorized away and made conceptually impossible. Reality is denuded of all value, making it insuperably difficult, if not impossible, for individuals to adjudicate between different values – discriminations, even of the most sophisticated kind, appear arbitrary and self-serving. The conflation of value with choice results in the following, overdetermined, dichotomous alternatives: either we return values to reality and accept them as entirely determined, or we attribute them to the individual and accept them as entirely free. We appear to only have two options: either value is wholly determined by an objective reality or it is freely created by an unfettered subjectivity. That these appear as our only options and the first option is so difficult to establish produces reliance on a form of relativism as an unsatisfactory default position.

Murdoch traces the conflation of value with choice through 'the existentialist line' so as to demonstrate that it is *not*, even with modification, the philosophy that humanity requires (*MGM*, p. 133; *SG*, p. 46).[10] Murdoch's class of existentialists is wide-ranging. She includes philosophers such as Jean-Paul Sartre who claim the title; analytic moral philosophers such as Stuart Hampshire, R.M. Hare and A.J. Ayer;[11] and 'extreme existentialists' such as Fyodor Dostoevsky and Jacques Derrida, who 'in a reaction of thought' turn towards determinism (*SG*, pp. 35, 36).[12] Murdoch defines existentialism as any philosophy that exaggerates the freedom of the subject at the expense of the determinacy of reality or, inversely, exaggerates the determinacy of reality, at the expense of the subject's freedom. She reasons that both alternatives induce exalted suffering and produce irresponsibility. These positions induce an exalted suffering because in the first case individuals identify with having too much freedom (an unrealistic conception of will)[13] and in the second case individuals identify with having no freedom (an unrealistic conception of reality). In either case, irresponsibility is produced because the individual is either completely independent from reality (and therefore not required to determine and respond to its legitimate determinations of her), or she is entirely subject to it (and therefore not required to exert herself in determining it).

In both cases the term 'reality' is something of a misnomer because what is taken to be reality is in effect fantasy. We know it to be a fantasy for two reasons. First, it falsely unifies reality, robbing it of its complexity and difficulty, making it 'over-optimistic and romantic' (*SG*, p. 54). Second, it exaggerates the self as either completely free or constrained, when realistically, the 'self is a correspondingly smaller and less interesting object' (*SG*, pp. 67–8). Existentialism, in its straightforward and deterministic forms, fails to recognize what Murdoch and philosophical romanticism, as I present it, are so intent on having us appreciate: namely, that the individual is both determined and determining. This insight should be basic to any proper understanding of the human aspiration to become better. For it is an individual's desire to determine reality correctly (according to how it, and we, really are) that not only directs her attention to the determination of her desires by reality, but gives her licence to be more vulnerable to being determined – for this is the best way to ensure that how one determines reality reflects what reality is most like.

It is the failure of existentialism to appreciate the determining and determined nature of human beings, that compels Murdoch to describes the existentialist as having 'moved out of the shadowy region of *eikasia* as far as the fire, which he takes as his sun', explaining that 'the bright flickering light of the fire suggests the disturbed and semi-enlightened ego which is pleased and consoled by its discoveries, but still essentially self-absorbed, not realizing that the real world is somewhere else' (*EM*, p. 423). Being so absorbed with the inner life of the subject, existentialists forget the *revelatory* potential of the subject's relationship to the natural and social environment, and so lose sight of *moral truth* as the goal of a refined subjectivity. We are left with 'an irresponsible and undirected self-assertion which goes easily hand in hand with some brand of pseudo-scientific determinism' (*SG*, p. 48).

Murdoch criticizes existentialism for its overly romanticized conception of subjective freedom or determinism, referring to it as 'romantic provocation' or 'optimistic romancing' (*SG*, pp. 47, 72).[14]

Murdoch's censure of existentialism is empirical, philosophical and ethical. It is empirical because she thinks that it is not an accurate description of life, in that we do not experience ourselves in this way. It is philosophical because she is not convinced by its arguments. It is ethical because she believes that individuals *should not* conceive of themselves in this way (*SG*, p. 9). She highlights the ethically threatening nature of existentialism by referring to it as 'something positively Luciferian' (*SG*, p. 72). Murdoch formulates this ethical concern in terms of the existentialist denial of the doctrine of original sin (*SG*, p. 47).

Murdoch's reconciliation to philosophical romanticism

The doctrine of original sin refers to our universal ' "fallen" human condition' and the 'infinite difficulty' or, alternatively, our 'necessary fallibility' in apprehending a reality that is '*magnetic but inexhaustible*' (*SG*, pp. 28, 23, 42). To have fallen is to exist in relationship to 'an ideal limit of love or knowledge which always recedes' (*SG*, p. 28). Murdoch is using the term, 'original sin', ironically, for although she asserts that it is a 'synthetic *a priori* truth' she wants to ward off the attribution of any metaphysical privilege by pointing to the idea's fictional or mythical status (*SG*, p. 28). She approves Søren Kierkegaard's observation that when an ethic ignores sin it becomes a science, but when it acknowledges sin 'it is *eo ipso* beyond its sphere' (*SG*, p. 47). Here Murdoch draws attention to the simultaneous necessity and difficulty of a philosophical acknowledgement of original sin: it must acknowledge sin to be meaningful, but to do so is to move beyond argument in the direction of religion.

Murdoch's conclusion that the doctrine of original sin is true – that reality is 'magnetic but inexhaustible' – is based on an argument from experience or what she refers to as an act of faith. Reality seems to be like this whenever you look at it.[15] She accepts that to be human is to be 'a unified being who sees, and who desires in accordance with what he sees, and who has some continual slight control over the direction and focus of vision' (*SG*, p. 40). All that is left for us is to try to 'see justly, to overcome prejudice, to avoid temptation, to control and curb imagination, to direct reflection' (*SG*, p. 40). Although Murdoch acknowledges that this is not a new idea, she thinks that philosophy consistently fails to appreciate its moral import because it refuses to accept 'a darker, less fully conscious, less steadily rational image of the dynamics of human personality' (*SG*, pp. 43–4). Seeing ourselves and others is much more difficult than philosophy presumes. Murdoch attributes the modern formulation of this view to Sigmund Freud's pessimistic view of human nature. He sees the psyche as

> an egocentric system of quasi-mechanical energy, largely determined by its own individual history, whose natural attachments are sexual, ambiguous, and hard for the subject to understand or control. Introspection reveals only the deep tissue of ambivalent motive, and fantasy is a stronger force than reason. (*SG*, p. 51)[16]

Realism depends on a commitment to becoming less egocentric. In other words, an individual must overcome her fantasies and personal obsessions if she is going to see reality more truthfully; she must discipline her self-protecting fantasy mechanism in an effort to see others, including herself, more clearly. A commitment to realism is also necessary for goodness because an individual needs to see others truthfully in order to recognize their claim upon her. Both commitments are reflected in our effort to overcome the ego.

A significant point about original sin is that no amount of individual effort will, *on its own*, produce desired realism. Becoming better by pursuing the right values is not solely up to the individual. Murdoch formulates it as '*Good, not will, is transcendent*' (*SG*, p. 69). In curbing her egoistic determination of reality and making herself available to the determination of her values by reality, the individual comes to depend upon a reality that exceeds her determinative powers. The individual deconstructs her egoistic fantasy mechanism *in the hope that* she will be rewarded with a more truthful outlook (*SG*, p. 63). The individual who resists the egoism of her perspective is analogous to the religious believer who 'feels that he needs, and can receive, extra help. "Not I, but Christ"' (*SG*, p. 83). It is as an act of faith, for whether the individual's efforts at rectifying her perspective are to be rewarded depends on contingent events; it depends on the grace of the gods. Grace need not be thought of in a strictly religious sense, for it can simply refer to an 'availability of supplementary energy' (*SG*, p. 83); the idea of 'supernatural assistance to human endeavour which overcomes empirical limitations of personality' (*SG*, p. 55).

Original sin and grace are Murdoch's formulations of the underlying thought – Kant's original Copernican Revolution – that humans cannot know the reality that grounds existence, *including that of their own*. Recognizing our inability to know reality entails that we accept the absolute pointlessness of human life or, alternatively, its 'utter lack of finality' (*SG*, p. 71). Murdoch writes that 'human life has no external, guaranteed or general pattern', not even of a secular, romantic kind (*SG*, p. 79). We are what we seem to be, transient mortal creatures subject to necessity and chance' (*SG*, p. 79). There is nothing a priori about humanity that saves us: not suffering freedom, not creative genius and not radical determinism. This is the intended meaning behind Murdoch's claim that there are no quasi-metaphysical substitutes for God. To think of humanity as redeemed by a higher calling, purpose or faculty is just mistaken self-importance or hubris – Murdoch says that ' "all is vanity" is the beginning and end of ethics' (*SG*, p. 71). Yet, she argues, it is this recognition of our nothingness that is the best, if not only, motivation for our wanting to respond appropriately to other individuals in their nothingness. She writes that

> The only genuine way to be good is to be good 'for nothing' in the midst of a scene where every 'natural' thing, including one's own mind, is subject to chance, that is, to necessity. That 'for nothing' is indeed the experience correlate of the invisibility or non-representable blankness of the idea of Good itself. (*SG*, p. 71)

We can now see that Murdoch uses the term 'romantic' or 'romanticism' to refer to a deep desire on the part of consciousness to avoid confronting the reality that 'all is vanity' and that humanity is 'for nothing'. Consciousness would prefer to accept anything, irrespective of whether it is consciousness, language, art or God, as the necessary and absolute measure of all life. Murdoch is critical of traditional religion and its secular equivalents (romanticism, existentialism and post-structuralism) for seeking solace in such 'objective' measures as God, reason and imagination. Although well-intentioned, and apparently inclusive, these 'objective' measures are elitist and result in the derision of ordinary consciousness – one of Murdoch's chief complaints. They cause us to overlook the universal and innocuous character of the moral effort to integrate transcendent reality into consciousness.

It is against the background of this critique that Murdoch represents herself as developing a philosophy that follows the tradition of the 'great romantics'. Her relationship to philosophical romanticism, proper – and analytic moral philosophy for that matter – is far more sympathetic and sophisticated than her criticisms indicate. She represents analytic moral philosophers as choosing to focus exclusively on conventional morality: 'when we pay our bills or perform other small everyday acts, we are just "anybody" doing what is proper or making simple choices for ordinary public reasons' (*SG*, p. 43). Philosophical romanticism considers private morality of 'the individual in pursuit of the individual ... responding to the magnetic pull of the idea of perfection' (*SG*, p. 43). Murdoch's middle position argues for greater interplay of public and private morality. Her view is that the perspectives of romanticism and analytic moral philosophy, although not entirely mistaken, would each benefit from dialogue with the other.[17] For example, analytic moral philosophy treats conventional morality is if it were straightforward, when it is definitely not: 'the quaintly phrased hymn which I sang in my childhood, "Who sweeps a room as for Thy laws makes that and the action fine", was not talking foolishly' (*SG*, p. 43). Romanticism's treatment of private morality overlooks the times when an individual acts in accordance with conventional morality.

Romanticism and analytic moral philosophy ignore precisely what Murdoch is intent on emphasizing, namely that 'the task of attention goes on all the time and at apparently empty and everyday moments we are "looking", making those little peering efforts of imagination which have such important cumulative results' (*SG*, p. 43). She defends the romantic paradigm, but only in its extension to conventional morality: romantics need to abandon their images of isolation and grandeur so as to witness the much less heroic and more innocuous occasions of imaginative peering. If they are going to do justice to the moral life, romantics must recognize that mothers romanticize the world, students romanticize the world and individuals who take pleasure in tending to pets and potted plants romanticize the world. According to Murdoch, the romantics' inability to appreciate less dramatic occasions of imaginative peering is partly a result of its masculine bias. Although Murdoch makes only oblique reference to the role of gender, in philosophical thought – when she comments that Freud 'was too much of an all-male grandee to appreciate' sado-masochism, and so was unable to diagnose its operation culturally – she remains highly conscious of its pervasiveness (*MGM*, p. 132). In particular, she actively works against the prototypically masculine romantic protagonist, independent, isolated, intensely dedicated to his art, in the possession of a muse, and an explorer of new and dangerous territories. She juxtaposes images endemic to romanticism (such as the individual observing the kestrel and the virtuous, seemingly unreflective peasant) with the conventional mother and daughter-in-law example and daily domestic chores (such as sweeping the floor, paying the bills and potting plants). That juxtaposition demonstrates how entrenched a particular instantiation of romantic thought has become: we mistake the illustration of romanticism for the thought itself, failing to see that it is one possible example of romanticizing the world among many more.

Murdoch rejects this masculine reductionism for two reasons. First, it results in elitism: it encourages individuals to conceive of their lives on the model of a work of art with the most authentic life being that of the artist or philosopher-poet. Murdoch accepts that some perspectives are more truthful than others and some individuals are wiser than others, arguing that this is because all perspectives participate in the truth; we are all, each and every one of us, truth-seekers. In Murdoch's view, there is no such thing as an 'unexamined' life, only plural possibilities for what the examined life is like, from Socrates to the peasant. By conceiving of each individual according to their relationship to the truth, she democratizes romanticism as much as she domesticates it. The second reason for her rejection of masculine romanticism is that it causes us to overlook and, in overlooking, hurt those individuals in our society who have less visibility – such as children, mothers, volunteers, neighbours and social workers. It makes these individuals even more invisible, which is problematic from Murdoch's point of view, because these invisible individuals are the really virtuous people in our community.

The contrast between individual visibility and invisibility is a philosophical and ethical issue for Murdoch. It is a philosophical issue because she thinks that romanticism, properly understood, *entails* an appreciation for the ordinary and everyday; a recognition of one's self as relational and required to be attentive to others. If the view that 'a saint described is a saint romanticized' is true, then it follows that genuine saints 'must be invisible both to others and to themselves' (*MGM*, p. 126). It is in defence of this point that Murdoch introduces humility, as opposed to sincerity or irony, as the penultimate virtue (as there is no ultimate virtue). The contrast between individual visibility and invisibility is an ethical issue for Murdoch because she thinks that individuals become virtuous by becoming like these invisible individuals. Her concern is that the masculinist, romantic paradigm encourages visibility, by appealing to our desire to be recognized and affirmed by those around us – in much the same way that falling in love has this effect. Romanticism persuades us that we are doing something important by creating ourselves; it allows us to feel good about ourselves as engaged in an ultimate human achievement.

Murdoch does not share the romantic's emphatic endorsement of *Bildung*. She argues that self-creation is necessary, but only to the extent that it enables the individual to accept her own inconsequence and respond to a reality that exceeds her understanding of it. Given the insuperable psychological difficulty involved in accepting our own nothingness, Murdoch is not surprised that romanticism should seek self-reassurance in a new categorical imperative requiring that the individual continually perfect herself. Such a categorical imperative, as with all categorical imperatives, allows us to exist in denial of our own death and nothingness; a categorical imperative enables individuals to dignify themselves through the heroic fulfilment of its absolute requirements. Imperatives that reflect our nothingness are incomplete and define our human condition as 'fallen'. If an ethical imperative can be derived from Murdoch's moral philosophy, it is to be receptive and 'cultivate' occasions for 'the siege of the individual by concepts' (*SG*, p. 32). This is not because it constitutes an end – this is the mistake made by the romantics – but because it facilitates a more truthful relationship *with reality*.

To curb egoism is to be suspicious of any theory that allows us to feel better about ourselves; it is to become more open to the formlessness of reality in one's desire to be determined by it. The cumulative result is a profound humbling of the self, as evidenced by the 'invisibility' of genuinely good people. They are not heroic or grand but tend to hide their wisdom in relationships with others (*MGM*, p. 115). The good person is, Murdoch writes, more likely to be 'consumed in anonymous work' (*MGM*, p. 115). The good individual recognizes that it is others, and not the self, who are most real, and that it is only by involving herself with what is other – that which resists the clamour of consciousness, like other individuals, language, academic studies, good art and literature – that her consciousness will be determined and determining in the right way. Murdoch concludes that humility is the penultimate virtue because 'although [the humble man] is not by definition the good man perhaps he is the kind of man who is most likely of all to become good' (*SG*, p. 104).

In a correction to the masculinist paradigm of romanticism, Murdoch represents humility as a clear improvement upon the romantic concept of irony. Romantic irony is an acknowledgement of inevitable human finitude in the effort to realize absolute infinity. The expression of romantic irony is a finely balanced achievement and – as with so many of the Aristotelian virtues – directs attention back to the individual as a cause for self-congratulation. The ironist develops an ability to explicitly highlight the partiality of her perspective as it seeks for universality, turning it into a source of pride. Humility is not something which we express, develop or achieve. It is simply an attitude that follows from an individual's recognition that 'all is vanity' and that 'the only way to be good is to be good "for nothing".' This is the meaning behind Murdoch's claim that humility and *not* irony, reveals an 'epistemology of the loving intellect' (*MGM*, p. 115). To accept the determination of consciousness by an undetermined reality is love. The knowledge produced by love is not ironic self-criticism, although this is a potential means, but a 'selfless respect for reality' (*SG*, p. 95). Murdoch is clear that 'humility is not a peculiar habit of self-effacement' because she is thinking of it epistemically, on the model of romantic irony, rather than psychologically (*SG*, p. 95).

Humility is one feature that distinguishes both Plato and Kant as 'great romantics'. In the tradition of philosophical romanticism, Plato and Kant are passionately interested in the determinative, receptive and transformative nature of human consciousness. Human consciousness lies at the centre of their philosophies that are dedicated to describing the character of human consciousness, its ability to approximate towards truth and the role of experiences in its transformative reorientation. Plato and Kant are unique in their refusal to remain at the level of human consciousness – what Murdoch refers to as the fire – for they do not derive such reassuring imperatives as ironical distance combined with ongoing self-improvement. Their profound interest in human consciousness is tempered by an equally profound sense of its limits, not just in terms of its determinative power, but, more importantly, in terms of its value or importance for us as human beings. Plato and Kant insist that human consciousness must be responsive and answerable to transcendent reality in the interests of an aspiration to become good and know the truth. Without an objective ground for our existence, human beings are singularly beholden to experiential intimations of what is most real, for it is only these occasions that are genuinely capable of pointing us in the right direction. Plato and Kant retain their faith in the possibility of goodness and truthfulness, but humbly acknowledge that it is less a matter of individual achievement and more a matter of grace.

Connected with Murdoch's conception of humility is her assertion that the inconsequential and the comic are more profound threats to human consciousness than evil and ignorance (although these are obviously important). She is enunciating two worries. First, she is concerned that to revile evil and ignorance is simply to condemn those individuals and communities thought to perpetuate them. Second, she is concerned that fear of despair is motivated by a desire for its glory (i.e. that we are replacing death with suffering). Death threatens us with the inconsequential, pathos and the comic, for pathos and comedy confront us with the meaninglessness of human life. This idea can be illustrated by considering what humility risks that irony does not. The humble individual, unlike the ironist, is *not* secure in her attitude of hyper-self-criticism and ongoing self-revision, because she appreciates the need and the difficulty involved in responding to what is other to the fantasy mechanism of the self – she has more to lose in not allowing her consciousness to be determined by a reality that exceeds her comprehension. The humble individual seeks to encounter the genuinely new, but to do so risks appearing ridiculous, inconsequential, foolish, pathetic and awkward.

Murdoch sometimes seems to say, particularly in her fiction, that being the subject of derision, ridicule and humiliation is the mark of humility. There are many reasons why humility engenders this response. First, the humble individual already accepts the 'for nothingness' and so has little investment in appearing superior to, or having authority over, other individuals; for it is such achievements as these that feed a false sense of our own self-importance. Neither is she a masochist who plays the role of a victim in order to fulfil another's need to feel self-important. Rather she tries to respond to individuals, cultures or disciplines, *as she finds them*, and not in terms of how she or they are inclined to understand themselves. Such an enterprise invites mistakes: mistakes produced by misunderstandings (we are not accustomed to interacting in these ways); mistakes produced by not knowing how to go on; and mistakes produced by misidentification of the new or real (represented in Murdoch's fiction by people falling in and out of love). Murdoch's own commitment to philosophical and personal humility is demonstrated in the following ways: her preparedness to work as a philosopher and a novelist; her use of religious language to enunciate ideas in an analytical, philosophical discourse; her childlike relationship with John Bayley; her liberal sexual morality; and conscientiously responding to all letters sent to her, irrespective of who they were from.

Conclusion

Murdoch's philosophy is less susceptible to her own criticisms of romanticism and more susceptible to others' criticisms of, specifically, literary romanticism. For example, T.S. Eliot accused literary romanticism of wallowing in the personal at the expense of a due respect for social convention and order (Eldridge 2001, p. 5). The same can be said of Murdoch's philosophy, in particular *The Sovereignty of Good*. Romanticism is accused of promoting a sympathy that is too large and the same can be said of Murdoch's philosophy. Both the romantics and Murdoch, have been charged with holding an apolitical conception of the imagination.[18] Their philosophies are thought to constitute an evasion of social reality. This objection is typified in Hans-Georg Gadamer's criticisms of Kant's *Critique of Judgement*. Nevertheless, both Murdoch's and the romantics' commitment to the transcendence of the political and the social is expressed through their faithfulness to our immersion in interpretive possibilities – that ambiguity is our final limit. This belief is reflected in their refusal to accept any one interpretation – in this case social/political – as the ultimate ground of explanation. As Geoffrey Hartman observes, there is 'a resistance to stable envisioning' in romantic thought (Eldridge 2001, p. 5).[19] Romantics resist an authoritative doctrine of value.

In his criticism of philosophical romanticism, D.Z. Phillips argues that the standards of philosophy disqualify it as philosophically illegitimate and incoherent. He argues that philosophical romanticism advocates a specific picture of human beings rather than adjudicating between different pictures. It pictures human beings 'as continuous self-interrogators and bearers of aspiration', on the basis of personal conviction rather than any sort of argument (Phillips 2002, p. 270). This tendency in philosophical romanticism has the effect of producing its own kind of dogma, foreclosing on other possibilities and precluding disagreement. Philosophical romanticism refuses to see 'that the moral demands on a philosophical writer involve him in doing conceptual justice to moral views other than his own' (p. 279) It is in order to determine whether these criticisms of philosophical romanticism – in particular those of D.Z. Phillips – apply in the case of Murdoch that I give a fuller elucidation of her romantic vision in the next chapter.

Chapter 5

Murdoch's Romantic Vision

Introduction

The purpose of this chapter is to elucidate a vision of Murdoch's philosophical romanticism. In the tradition of philosophical romanticism, Murdoch's philosophy does justice to the thought that 'there is more than this' without contradicting the inevitable perspectivity of our subjectivity. Her philosophy honours both human subjectivity and the all-too-human sense of a reality that transcends human subjectivity as necessary elements in the paradoxical situation that is our humanness. The epistemic and ethical task for individuals is to realize the infinite in the finite, giving simultaneous expression to the task's final incompleteness. I introduce Murdoch's philosophical romanticism with an analysis of her concept of the sublime. I develop my analysis through a discussion of what Murdoch means by the terms, 'egoism' and 'love', concluding that she attributes two senses to each term ('egoism' and 'Egoism'; 'love' and 'Love') that require differentiation if her philosophy is not to be misconstrued. I argue that for Murdoch, as with philosophical romanticism, *learning* – the pilgrimage from appearance to reality – is constitutive of, and the uniquely appropriate response to, the paradoxical situation which is our humanness. Further, it is by way of appreciating this hypothetical imperative that ethical interpersonal relationships become possible.

The sublime as a theory of tragedy[1]

Romanticism defines a particular heroic illusion of exalted suffering and isolated creativity that is typified by the variants of romanticism: existentialism, analytic moral philosophy and deconstruction. In her novels, Murdoch contrasts the heroic and self-important subject of romanticism with fictional protagonists that are comic, incompetent, unattractive, hopelessly well-intentioned, fantasy-ridden, vulnerable and inadequate.[2] These characters 'partake of the funniness and absurdity and contingent incompleteness and lack of dignity of people in ordinary life' (*MGM*, p. 97). They lack 'formal wholeness', mirroring the messiness of real people, that we are 'unfinished and full of blankness and jumble; only in our own illusioning fantasy are we complete' (*MGM*, p. 97).

Murdoch aims to represent characters that are contingent, historical, messy, free and separate individualized centres of meaning. It is imperative for her that these characters do not appear either as elements in her own self-dramatizing myth or as representatives of different conventional outlooks. Murdoch aspires to authorial tolerance, signified by the creation of characters that are 'mutually independent centres of significance' (*EM*, p. 271). Such tolerance, she thinks, distinguishes great writers, the greatest of which is William Shakespeare.[3] This 'godlike' tolerance, which Murdoch more aptly describes as love, involves the recognition 'that something real exists other than oneself' (*EM*, p. 264). It involves a disciplined and arduous transcendence of our fears: of 'history, real beings, and real change, whatever is contingent, messy, boundless, infinitely particular, and endlessly still to be explained; what is desired is the timeless non-discursive whole which has its significance completely contained in itself' (*EM*, p. 274).

These fears effectively involve the limits of consciousness, intelligibility and representation: that is, we fear what it is that we cannot determine or make sense of. We also fear whatever happens to ridicule and emasculate the pursuit of meaning, like absurdity, for example. Murdoch shows us that chance rules our destinies more than we care to acknowledge. In the language of one commentator, she would have us see that 'we are absurd creatures rather than protagonists who struggle against destiny with tragic seriousness' (Gordon 2001, p. 14). To disengage our fear of the limits of consciousness is, in Murdoch's view, to confront death and chance; it is to appreciate the absolute contingency of all conceptual understanding. The individual effectively recognizes that the way in which she pictures reality is subject to the particularities and details of her life, is just one among many pictures and is capable of transformation, modification and ultimate substitution.

This confrontation with death and chance is critical for two reasons. First, it shifts the limit of consciousness from that of the determinant, or known, to the indeterminant or unknown. It allows the individual's form-making consciousness to be shaped and directed by the formlessness of a transcendent reality in which she is immersed, resulting in a freer and more truthful subjectivity.[4] Peter Conradi, Murdoch's biographer and commentator, evokes this shift in the limit of consciousness by referring to an 'exposure to the world's particular ... in which the box-like enclosure of the self is attenuated and opened out' (2001, p. 138). Consciousness, realizing that it is not everything, allows itself to be determined by a reality which surrounds it but exceeds its powers of comprehension. The individual is receptive to experiences that are not made palatable by form-giving consciousness in an effort to be compelled by something other than consciousness.

This is the meaning behind Murdoch's reference to the selflessness of objective consciousness. She uses the term 'unselfing' in the context of her discussions of death (meta-ethics) rather than desire (moral psychology), although the two are obviously related. 'Unselfing', as Murdoch intends it, does not involve a repudiation of one's own perspective or interests for that matter, with a retreat into the view from nowhere; it is not static, mechanical or aperspectival.[5] Rather, 'unselfing' involves an acceptance of one's own perspective as inherently limited – embraced as personal, historical, provisional and incomplete – in an embrace of what is not-consciousness. If anything is abandoned, it is an illusion of the self as inviolably important and master of everything that it surveys.

Second, this reorientation of consciousness uniquely engenders a recognition of other individuals as centres of meaning; as being subjects like ourselves.[6] Although other individuals are found to be radically separate and exquisitely precious, our relationship with them need not be defined by selflessness or altruism (although there may be occasions for each). Rather, the relationship is defined by trust. Individuals engage with another in a spirit of mutual acceptance and intersubjective determination. Mutually vulnerable, individuals accept mutual transformation as they labour to understand one another. Individuals recognize that each determines the other and that these determinations are incomplete and infinitely perfectible. They continually correct and deepen their mutual determinations of one another, with the view to reflecting the mysterious, dynamic, mutually affecting relationship that exists between them.

It is important to note that such an approach to interpersonal relationships does not guarantee their success or endurance. There are surprise events that relationships may not be able to accommodate, such as the death of a child, an infidelity, a false accusation, an accident, or the relocation of a family.[7] Further, contrary to their best intentions, people slip back into pictures that are familiar, although distorting. Murdoch's fiction is typified by the advances, conflicts and setbacks of her characters and their relationships with one another. Her characters are made to repeat themselves endlessly and irrationally for the reason that 'the unconscious delights in identifying people with each other. It has only a few characters to play with' (Conradi 2001, p. 101). Reasonableness is not innately given, but 'has to be earned, unendingly struggled for' (Conradi 2001, p. 21). And for this struggle individuals require certain myths, as much as they need to repudiate others. As with the novelist, we 'must use myth and magic to help liberate us from myth and magic' (Conradi 2001, p. 28).

To return to Murdoch's original statement of authorial love: it employs a modified and, some might argue, improved version of the Kantian sublime. Kant introduces the sublime as an experience when individuals are confronted by the limits of their representative powers of imagination. This limit to the representative impulse is occasioned by natural magnitude (mathematical sublime) and force (dynamical sublime). According to Kant, it is the sheer size and force of nature that ominously overshadows humanity's purposefulness, in both a literal and metaphorical sense. Nature powerfully dwarfs and, in some cases, devastates human achievement (engineering, architecture, art, towns, etc.) As a spectacle, nature's expansive magnitude and excessive force represent a limit to human imagination and understanding. Contrary to expectation perhaps, the individual does not cower in fear before the dramatic confrontation with the limits of consciousness. Instead, the individual feels intense exhilaration in the discovery that the real limit to consciousness is elsewhere.

The concept of the sublime is significant for Kant because it prompts an intuition of the self as, *in reality*, moral. An individual's sense of himself is heightened, as opposed to being diminished, by his confrontation with nature's vast magnitude and strength – he discovers his true identity in practical reason. Although humans are part of nature, they experience themselves as significant in their separation from it. This idea is reflected in the thinking of romanticism, particularly the paintings of Casper David Friedrich. His paintings characteristically depict the human subject in a natural environment which is vast and/or threatening in order to illustrate how the inclusion of human subjectivity alters the significance of nature. Natural magnitude and powers become symbolic externalizations of internal consciousness and freedom, dignifying instead of dwarfing humanity. Observers of romantic paintings witness the painful inadequacy and defencelessness of human beings, as well their profound majesty that surpasses, as it is accentuated by, their natural vulnerability. It is through the sublime that the 'objective reality' of nature undergoes important modifications as it is understood in relation to the 'subjectivity' of the individual.

Murdoch lauds Kant for his concept of the sublime, accusing him of wrongly locating it in a dichotomous relationship between nature (mechanism) and reason (deliberation). She writes that Kant attaches the sublime, a concept so pregnant with significance, to a relatively 'trivial occasion', and that we need to 'think of the spectator as gazing not at the Alps, *but at the spectacle of human life*' (*EM*, pp. 264, 282, emphasis added). Sublimity, according to Murdoch, is the experience of sharing our surroundings with other individuals: 'It is the spectacle of this manifold, if we can actually apprehend it, which is not easy, which brings the exhilaration and the power and reminds us, to use Kant's words, of our supersensible destiny' (*EM*, p. 282). Kant also mistakenly associates sublimity with feelings of superiority attributed to the presence and intuition of reason: the individual feels overwhelming awe *for himself* as a free and moral agent.

Murdoch's criticism of Kant is that he allows the a priori and 'guaranteed pattern' of reason to save humankind (*SG*, p. 79). Human beings are redeemed, not by God but by reason. Murdoch's objections are logical and epistemological. She thinks an implication of Kant's Copernican Revolution is that nothing a priori (not even reason) can justify and save humanity from being more than 'transient mortal creatures subject to necessity and chance' – neither God nor any of the substitutes for God (*SG*, p. 79). The establishment of reason as pre-eminently sovereign conflicts with the founding insight of Kant's critical philosophy, namely, that we *cannot* determine the absolute foundation of human consciousness. Murdoch draws on Platonic imagery to articulate this idea with reference to the Good. She writes that

> While it seems proper to represent the Good as a centre or focus of attention, yet it cannot quite be thought of as a 'visible' one in that it cannot be experienced or represented or defined. We can certainly know more or less where the sun is; it is not so easy to imagine what it would be like to look at it. (*SG*, p. 70)

Epistemically speaking, Murdoch accuses Kant of substituting suffering for death. His conception of the sublime consoles us as it appeals to our sado-masochistic tendencies; it introduces a mythical limit to consciousness in the form of *a priori* reason, consoling us by imposing 'pattern upon something which might otherwise seem intolerably chancy and incomplete' (*SG*, p. 87). The Kantian sublime appeals to our sado-masochistic tendencies because it allows us to *play at* a confrontation with our existential fears while masquerading as purification. The Kantian sublime is 'a violent mock-ascesis or false loss of self' (Conradi 2001, p. 141). It is a contrivance that serves self-understanding: the individual engages in a self directed enjoyment of nature only to experience her own superiority over that nature. As with 'falling in love', this apotheosis or sense of superiority is effectively empty: it does not guide the individual in her exercise of reason. As an empty ideal, it is susceptible to illusory 'completion', as in the case of existentialist philosophy and the assertion that humans are radically free.

Murdoch argues, in contrast to Kant, that the discovery of oneself as moral, *appropriately understood*, inspires humility rather than awe or superiority. Murdoch says that the individual she has in mind, when 'faced by the manifold of humanity, may feel, as well as terror, delight, but not, if he really sees what is before him, superiority. He will suffer an undramatic, un-selfcentred, agnosticism which goes with tolerance' (*EM*, p. 283). This is because the real threat to representational consciousness is not nature, as excess, but the inherent formlessness of reality. It is insuperably difficult, if not impossible, for human beings to imagine or conceive existence as contingent (*MGM*, p. 144).[8] Consciousness unifies reality such that it is impossible to have an unmediated, unpatterned comprehension of the real; human beings routinely 'round off' situations and 'sum up' characters (*EM*, p. 285). This epistemic constraint has a psychological dimension, as our psychological tendency is 'to conceal death and chance by the invention of forms' (*SG*, p. 87).[9] Individuals rely on, and inadvertently determine, their unifying worldviews and summaries of others, so as to provide themselves with a sense of purpose, comfort, personal aggrandizement, consolation and reconciliation to one's fate.

The process by which we overcome such reliance is inherently moral. It involves addressing 'relentlessly strong selfish forces ... which we scarcely comprehend' (*SG*, p. 99). To do this, we must

> *work*, using or failing to use our honesty, our courage, our truthful imagination, at the interpretation of what is present to us, as we of necessity shape it and 'make something of it'. We help it to be. We work at the meeting-point where we deal with a world which is other than ourselves. (*MGM*, p. 215)

Murdoch acknowledges that for individuals to be inspired to engage in a process which is psychologically difficult, morally exacting and only ever partially successful, they require experiences of the sublime – Kant was right in this regard. What he fails to appreciate is the true nature of sublimity. Sublime experiences involve an encounter with death, chance, and the reality of other individuals. By death, Murdoch does not mean 'a "terribly special" event at the end of life', but rather 'something that could happen all the time, in the sense of unselfing' (Conradi 2001, p. 123). Murdoch says that 'Goodness is connected with the acceptance of real death and real chance and real transience'; it is 'an acceptance of our own nothingness which is an automatic spur to our concern with what is not ourselves' (*SG*, p. 103).

Murdoch proposes that Kant's theory of the sublime 'be transformed into a theory of art' applicable to prose literature, and specifically, tragedy (*EM*, p. 282). Prose literature uniquely reveals the absolute contingency of human life combined with a necessity for truth and goodness.[10] Of all prose literature, tragedy does this best, through the creation of an artistic form that highlights inherent formlessness. The most important thing that novels do is illuminate 'that other people exist' (*EM*, p. 282). Tragedies and novels represent the sublime and are, as such, spiritual exercises. Their creation involves a struggle for freedom or 'virtuous knowing': being able to represent things 'quite other than ourselves' or, alternatively, 'apprehending that other people exist' (*EM*, p. 283). Murdoch concludes that

> The knowledge and imagination which is virtue is precisely the kind which the novelist needs to let his characters be, to respect their freedom, and to study them themselves in that most significant area of activity, where they are trying to apprehend the reality of others. The artist is indeed the analogon of the good man, and in a special sense he *is* the good man: the lover who, nothing himself, lets other things be through him. (*EM*, p. 284)

There is an important analogy here between Murdoch's philosophy and Kant's *Critique of Judgement*. The purpose of Kant's *Critique of Judgement* was to solve an impasse that he had created by his two earlier critiques. Put simply, but I hope not simplistically, in the *First Critique* Kant limits human knowledge and understanding to phenomenal experience and in the *Second Critique* he establishes that human beings are, as things-in-themselves, practically free. Because he restricts human understanding to phenomenal experience, he cannot give an account of how individuals intuit themselves as free or their environments as amendable to the exercise of their freedom. The sublime overcomes this impasse by providing individuals with an intuition or sense of themselves as free.

The sublime similarly overcomes an impasse in Murdoch's philosophy: Murdoch limits understanding to consciousness but, on the basis of the sublime, also asserts the reality of the Good. Individuals do not react to a confrontation with the limits of representative consciousness – death, chance, banality, the void or meaninglessness – in a predictable way. Instead of retreating deeper into one's own self-consoling, self-protecting, fantasies (as might be expected) the individual experiences the sublime as an educational sacrament or source of good energy. That is to say, in recognizing the contingency of her own perspective the individual is inspired to cultivate a more truthful, less illusory one by being open to other possibilities. What this response to the sublime reveals, according to Murdoch, is that the individual intuits herself as claimed by truth and goodness, in the very moment that she recognizes the impossibility of both. We can come to a better understanding of the role of the sublime in Murdoch's philosophy by examining her two senses of egoism and love.

Egoism and egoism: Murdoch's two fundamental assumptions

'Egoism' has two senses in Murdoch's moral philosophy. It is important to differentiate them so as to appreciate the full extent of Murdoch's argument. For example, Murdoch is *not* arguing that if individuals overcome selfishness (psychological egoism), they will see reality (i.e. overcome epistemic egoism). Neither is Murdoch's philosophy an argument for altruism, in that she is not advocating that individuals must love other individuals more than themselves if they are to behave morally towards them.[11] Epistemic egoism refers to our fallen human condition or, alternatively, the doctrine of original sin – which is Murdoch's version of Kant's Copernican Revolution. Human experience of reality is mediated by a consciousness that is interpretive, compelled to 'make classifications and set up analogies', and artistic (*MGM*, p. 86). As individuals, 'we constantly weave our experience into limited wholes (art works), as when we "tell our day" in a series of vignettes' (*MGM*, pp. 35–6). Human consciousness is perspectival. Individuals inevitably experience reality as having a form – with the void as a possible exception[12] – and the effect of these forms is to distort, as much as it reveals, reality. There is no escaping this feature of consciousness. It follows that humans are incapable of knowing reality directly – unmediated by form-giving consciousness – or in its entirety. We in effect guess as to the true nature of reality, from sparks, intimations and clues provided by the shadows (*MGM*, p. 124). Consciousness is therefore subject to 'an inevitable imperfection, or of an ideal limit of love or knowledge which always recedes' (*SG*, p. 28). This is Murdoch's first sense of what Egoism means: it is constitutive of our humanity as 'a synthetic a priori truth'.

As with Kant's critical philosophy, these artistic unities of consciousness serve to unify and stabilize the individual as much as they do reality. Murdoch writes that 'self, thing, person, story and work of art are wholes which can function as analogies of each other' (*MGM*, p. 147). It is possible therefore to intuit the self in a work of art as it is to intuit reality in a self – these unities imply or mirror one another. It is not surprising that these aesthetic unities, by which consciousness pictures and frames reality and a corresponding self, fulfil deep psychological needs. Although Murdoch's Freudian, Christian framework is perhaps less subtle and sophisticated than recent developments in contemporary materialist, feminist and poststructuralist discourses, her point is the same. Human subjectivity is dark, deep, opaque, obscure, complex, devious, messy, normally self-serving, consolation-seeking and vulnerable to self-deception. She writes that 'introspection reveals only the deep tissue of ambivalent motive, and fantasy is a stronger force than reason' (*SG*, p. 51). This is Murdoch's second sense of egoism.

Egoism, in this second sense, does not refer to humanity's selfish impulses that must be subordinated if we are to recognize the needs of others – Murdoch's philosophical psychology is more sophisticated than this. It refers to human personality, a less rational 'historically determined individual looking after itself' that is 'reluctant to face unpleasant realities' and 'constantly seeks consolation, either through imagined inflation of self or through fictions of a theological nature' (*SG*, pp. 78–9). Egoism of this sort produces 'a cloud of more or less fantastic reverie designed to protect the psyche from pain', readily allowing for 'false unity and multiplicity' (*MGM*, pp. 79, 165). Its love 'is normally too profoundly possessive and also too "mechanical" to be a place of vision' (*SG*, p. 75).

Combining Murdoch's two senses of egoism, it is apparent that the human psyche is significantly invested in the artistic unities of consciousness. The psyche wants to usurp control of consciousness directing it to create unities that allay egoistic anxieties, while at the same time preserving the psyche's sense of consciousness as truth-seeking. The operation of the human psyche is largely unconscious and it requires great moral effort on the part of the individual to bring it into consciousness. Consequently, although the unifying aesthetic forms of consciousness distort reality, some are more falsifying than others because they are more subject to the egoism of the human personality. The epistemic variation between different interpretive perspectives is relative to egoism in this sense: if the psyche is dominant then consciousness reveals more about ourselves than it does the world, and if the psyche is dormant then consciousness reveals more about the world than it does about ourselves (referred to by Murdoch as the selflessness of realism). The more subject consciousness is to the egoism of the human personality, the more misrepresentative its unifying forms will be, and vice versa.

Given that consciousness is truth-seeking and the psyche operates unconsciously, the individual must 'attempt to pierce the veil of selfish consciousness' (*SG*, p. 93). Individuals should vigilantly investigate the interpretive and whole-making forms of consciousness for any traces of the egoistic fantasy mechanism. This is illustrated in *The Sovereignty of Good* by the example of M and D (mother and daughter-in-law), for M overturns an earlier evaluation of D on the basis that it was rooted in her jealousy and desire to be socially accepted. M acknowledges that she is 'old-fashioned and conventional', stating, 'I may be prejudiced and narrow-minded. I may be snobbish. I am certainly jealous' (*SG*, p. 17). The example of M and D illustrates that it is through appreciating the psychological limitations of a perspective that the individual becomes capable of transcending and correcting it, having become receptive to what had once been excluded. In recognizing her prior perspective as closed *in particular ways*, M is opened to the possibility of a new, but not just any, perspective. M's second description of D implies greater vulnerability in her relationship with D; in this second description D is more capable of revealing to M facets of herself and others that she might not have otherwise discovered. M's second description of D is closer to her experience of D rather than to her expectations of her: M experiences D as spontaneous, gay and youthful. M's second description of D aspires to be true to D as M finds her.

An implication of M's second description of D is that the process is likely to be ongoing, for the more that M opens herself up to being determined by D, and not her expectations for what D should be like, the more likely it is that her description of D will change to reflect her evolving relationship with D. Iconoclasm is an apt description of the subject's continuous sorting of the idiosyncratic from the more objective elements of experience. As with religious icons and images, these pictures of consciousness have a powerful psychological hold, serving to energize, rationalize and protect us in the living of our lives. M cannot begin to revise her impressions of D until she honestly admits to, and confronts, her own conventionality and jealousy – this is not at all easy to do because her identity and worldview are at stake.

Murdoch formulates this distinction between true and false consciousness by way of the imagination: at one end of the spectrum there is 'trapped egoistic *fantasy*' and at the other end there is '*imagination* as a faculty of transcendence' (*MGM*, p. 86). She concludes that 'all of us are engaged in an ongoing struggle against those schizophrenic temptations to distort or exceed the imaginative limits within which human life is possible and fruitful' (*MGM*, p. 86). Murdoch defends her normative differentiation of transcendent-seeking imagination from fantasy on the grounds that it is operative in our evaluation of art. She claims that art 'presents the most comprehensible examples of the almost irresistible human tendency to seek consolation in fantasy and also of the effort to resist this' (*EM*, p. 353). Bad art is far more common than good art; it is self-consoling and self-aggrandizing fantasy; it is personal in the sense that the myths under which the author or artist operates are readily apparent; it frequently appeals to perverse forms of reality and the good by indulging humanity's sado-masochistic tendencies. In contradistinction to bad art, good art is rare and difficult to achieve; it is impersonal because the author or artist acts like an invisible presence; and 'we intuit our best selves in its mirror, and not only when we are under its spell ... Art sets us in order, the ideal unity of the object makes us also one' (*MGM*, p. 81).

Individuals evaluate works of art according to how the art object makes them feel, and how they feel is a function of what it does, and does not, enable them to see. As a consequence, Murdoch claims that 'a great deal of art, perhaps most art, actually is self-consoling fantasy, that is, *it does not teach*' (*SG*, p. 85; emphasis added). Bad art does not teach in that it does not produce learning in those who view it or read it. Learning, defined as 'the siege of the individual by concepts' is another of Murdoch's central concepts that I consider in the next section (*SG*, p. 32). Before proceeding, it is noteworthy that the perfectibility of art and consciousness is infinite – this defines our Egoism. It is our commitment to a transcendent reality and absolute truth that entails a lifetime devotion to provisional, shifting, imperfect, truthfulness as manifested in a constant overcoming of psychological egoism. Although human consciousness cannot know reality or the good, if it can transcend its own self-consoling fantasies, then it will be more prepared for, and more appreciative of, the intimations of reality and goodness available in human experience.

Learning: pedagogy of limits and new beginnings

Murdoch writes that '[the] whole person is a mixture of knowledge and illusion, immersed in a reality which transcends it, failing or succeeding to *learn*, in innumerable ways, the difference between true and false, good and evil' (*MGM*, pp. 153–4). Murdoch uses *learning* in a very specialized sense. She does not include what many of us take for granted as learning: learning that the bus is late or that it is going to rain tomorrow; and learning how to operate a computer, for example. She classifies these as instances of *knowing* because they do not involve a revision of consciousness in light of its discerned limits. Learning, in Murdoch's view, involves an encounter with the sublime, of which beauty can be an instance. Potential occasions of learning identified by Murdoch include: praying; being before a beautiful painting or landscape; being absorbed in an intellectual or creative activity; taking delight in potting plants; and enjoying the company of animals.

These likely occasions for learning are illustrative and not prescriptive because consciousness is personal and historical. The most common occasion of learning is also the most corruptible, namely falling in love (see next section). In learning, the limits of consciousness are in continual reconstitution as consciousness moulds itself to newly imagined possibilities, choreographically taking its cues from a reality that overflows its closure and withdraws into mystery; we are pointed in the direction of deepened understanding as consciousness seeks an alternative perspective that includes, but goes beyond, prior conceptual understanding. This is not merely an intellectual exercise because conceptual change involves, in the words of Wittgensteinian philosopher Cora Diamond, 'coming into life with that term, whose possibilities are to a great extent to be made', going on 'in ways that no one else would, expecting that others will follow what one has said' (Diamond 1988, p. 268). Having experienced something as exemplary, the individual aspires to emulate a reality that it is desirable but beyond immediate conceptual grasp. Consciousness undergoes a compulsory reorientation of perspective in light of an experience that is expressive of a normative understanding. The learning transforms the individual in, and through, her transformed engagement with reality. It describes a refocusing and reorientation of consciousness that can be spontaneous or evolutionary, self-initiated or other-initiated, desired or unexpected.

Learning is the mark of ethical subjectivity because it characterizes a consciousness that answers to a transcendent reality. It is in relationship to reality as transcendent, that concepts are infinitely learned. The learning subject repeatedly constantly understands a situation, person or history anew, coming to see it all, yet again, in a different light. It involves the constant re-description of reality and the constant retelling one's own story. The movement though is from selfishness – less reality – to unselfishness – more reality. Unselfishness refers to the transfiguration of an individual's desires in an embrace of an external, independent and infinite reality. The individual does not recognize what was once obscured, but learns 'that what we want is always "beyond"' (*EM*, p. 416). As Murdoch says, 'the instructed and morally purified mind sees reality clearly and indeed (in an important sense) *provides us with the concept*' (*EM*, p. 426).

Learning can, but need not, involve vigilant self-criticism, as in the case of M and D, for not everyone stops to look at fire on their way to the sun. It definitely involves *naïveté*: an openness to being claimed by the normative authority of new, anomalous, taken-for-granted experiences so as to allow them to 'capture our imagination'. For it is in an effort to answer to these new experiences that individuals invent new concepts and make new imperfect uses of old concepts. Although M does this in her re-description of D, the *naïveté* involved in learning is better illustrated, in *The Sovereignty of Good*, with Murdoch's example of the individual observing a kestrel in flight. I am going to call this individual K. K is staring out the window, in an 'anxious and resentful state of mind', preoccupied by an offence to her vanity, when suddenly she sees a 'hovering kestrel' (*SG*, p. 84). K reflects that 'In a moment everything is altered. The brooding self with its hurt vanity has disappeared. There is nothing now but kestrel' (*SG*, p. 84). When K returns to thinking about the other matter, is seems so much 'less important' (*SG*, p. 84).

Although K does not, in this instance, revise her previous assessment – whatever happened remains an offence to her vanity – the whole gestalt of such judgements is momentarily and, perhaps, irrevocably altered. K is compelled by the kestrel's effortless and joyful hovering to question her effort in the strain to preserve and protect her own prestige. K begins to wonder about whether prestige, given its tenuousness, is really that worthwhile and meaningful. Prior to the kestrel, K exists in a 'metaphysics' of the 'prestige' perspective: a world divided into individuals with and without prestige; a world divided between acts that do and do not promote prestige; a world divided between allies and enemies. She is incapable of 'seeing it [prestige] in perspective' without the prompting from an outside individual, experience or ritual that answers to, and exhibits, an alternative 'metaphysics' or conceptual set, which in the case of K was the effortless and joyful hovering of a kestrel.

As with Kant's Copernican Revolution it should be theoretically impossible for human beings to have such insights. If experience is framed by consciousness, and consciousness is framed by one's conceptual set, then, by definition, it should be inconceivable that an individual could discern a reality that is beyond either his conceptual set or consciousness. But we do! But we need to proceed carefully at this point. Murdoch is arguing that M and K transcend the 'metaphysics' of their respective conceptual sets by seeing their limits and having intimations of alternative, more truthful, conceptual sets. It is important to emphasize that they do not transcend the limits of consciousness and see reality. But neither do they merely substitute one conceptual set for another. M and K find the new conceptual set compelling in the sense that, they find it authoritative (it claims their imagination), and in the sense that it moves them in the direction of truth and reality. How is it possible to know this given that we are denied access to reality? We do not know it with any kind of certainty, but we trust that we are right, and we remain ever vigilant.

Individuals trust occasions experienced as inherently pedagogical in the hope of not being deceived; sublimity is associated with a disclosure, and not ellipsis, of meaning. Trust in the sublime is exhibited in an individual's perseverant search for new, more appropriate understandings. The trust is characterized by a faith in the pedagogical potential of the sublime and a vigilant regard for its distorting possibilities. The individual is both artist and philosopher, for although she takes occasions of sublimity seriously, she does not do so dogmatically or blindly. As much as the individual trusts the sublime, she also regards it with a certain degree of suspicion: remembering past experiences, the individual recognizes that although her current perspective feels more objective than her previous one, it is likely to be replaced by even more objective perspectives in the future. All that is available to us, as human beings, is continuous experimentation, criticism and the refiguring of patterns through further imaginative picturing.

Given the culture of trust and suspicion surrounding the sublime, individuals are compelled to test their new understandings in dialogue and interaction with one another. It is through interacting and speaking with others that I discover the limitations of newly found perspectives and intimations of deeper, more compelling perspectives – other people's distinctive perspectives and perceptions of situations also provide signs for the direction in which consciousness needs to proceed. Murdoch claims that 'learning takes place when such words are used, either aloud or privately, in the context of a particular act of attention' (*SG*, p. 43). If what I have learned is genuinely more objective, then it ought to be recognizable by others – not because it is the view from nowhere but because it speaks to our common reality, that is, it inhabits the perspectives of others from within.

Love and love

It could be argued that Murdoch's analysis of learning only raises the epistemic question, once removed. How do we know that the new conceptual understanding that the individual has been inspired to develop really is an improvement? Again, it is impossible to know with any certainty, but a significant feature in its favour is that it is the outgrowth of love. As with egoism, love has two senses, given Murdoch's reference to it in the context of her meta-ethics (Love) and her philosophical psychology (love) – with an analogous relationship between the two. The most accessible sense of love is its psychological one. It typically describes a form of attachment: either between parent and child, as in the case of filial love; or between friends, as in the case of Platonic love; or between sexually intimate individuals, as in the case of romantic love. Murdoch has romantic love in mind when she is describing psychological love, and her novels are filled with characters falling in and out of love. As Conradi notes, 'I know of no other writer who has evoked its [falling in love] symptoms, pathology and, in a sense, its phenomenology – the changes it induces in consciousness – with such brilliance' (2001, p. 106).

Murdoch does not accept Hume's sceptical argument that because falling in love makes an individual see another in a way that others, including her past and future selves, may not share, it therefore causes us to see things that are not there. Murdoch's view is that falling in love can be a source of insight, sharpening perception as opposed to colouring it. Falling in love, however, is not her principal interest. She is interested in it as a metaphor for *ascesis*, what Conradi refers to as 'loss of self, in which the contingency of all that is unself is momentarily revealed with a glorious and ambiguously sublime radiance. The centre of significance is violently ripped out of the dreamy ego and placed in another, who is suddenly perceived as shockingly separate' (2001, p. 141). Murdoch's cynicism about falling in love is reflected in her representation of it as false or mock-ascesis: the lover, readily falling back on the self, behaves badly if her love is not reciprocated or if it is reciprocated in a manner that is found wanting.

Human love, of this sort, is egoistic and is therefore a metaphor for the egoism of ordinary consciousness: both are personal, invented and subjective. Murdoch labels consciousness and love as 'personal' in order to accentuate their self-interested character. She classifies them as 'invented' in order to emphasize that normally not obedient to anything beyond the egoistic desires of the self. The determination of consciousness and love as 'subjective' highlights the fact that they are informed by the fantasy mechanism of the personality: people and objects act as either obstacles or instruments for the consolidation of an individual's personality. Within the context of ordinary consciousness and love, objects and persons take on false value because the value that they come to have is conditional upon their role in the consciousness of another individual – it is in terms of the self that others are considered and valued. It is imaginary because in reality there are many selves and, as a consequence, many centres of value.

The purification of ordinary love and consciousness in the direction of greater 'unselfing' brings me to Murdoch's second sense of the term, which is modelled on the first but refers, meta-ethically, to the relationship of consciousness to its imaginative unifying pictures and the embodiment of these pictures in the variegated surface of art, literature and life. To Love something, in this second sense, is to be compelled by it; it is to see it as 'a great source of revelation' (*MGM*, p. 85). It is to 'claim perfection' for the object of love, as we do in the case of the beautiful (*MGM*, p. 85). As exemplary, the object of our love inspires obedience, manifested in further rumination, reflection and enactment. As with falling in love, Love, in this second sense, is a source of good energy, a sacrament.

The sublime inspires Love, and it is this Love which provides evidence for the veracity of the experience and a reason to believe that we are genuinely learning and not just flitting from one perspective to another. This is because 'One cannot feel unmixed love for a mediocre moral standard any more than one can for the work of a mediocre artist' (*SG*, p. 62). To Love a moral standard, work of art, or idea is to consider it perfect, and 'for all our frailty the command "be perfect" has sense for us' (*SG*, p. 93). The introduction of this moral standard, work of art, or idea infuses our experiences with hierarchy, so that we can now see what we previously followed, valued or thought as flawed, petty, vain, superficial, sentimental, narrow-minded or fearful. In other words, it is in light of imagined perfection, that we have a conception of imperfection – this is Murdoch's version of the ontological argument. The existence of perfection is logically necessary if I am to have a conception of myself as imperfect.

Love, in this second sense, directs consciousness to seek reality that is outside its own limit; blindly to reach and seek for what it finds imaginatively compelling. Love is articulated through our everyday use of language. Murdoch writes that 'We are men and we are moral agents before we are scientists, and the place of science in human life must be discussed in *words*' (*SG*, p. 34). Language is used to express and clarify this newly emerging understanding. Words are more than just mere records of external reality; they are symptomatic of shifts in consciousness and release a human identity that is attached to aspirations as they come into articulation. Similarly with behaviour: it is not just a matter of deliberation and choice, but about shifts in consciousness as they reveal new possibilities for individuality and living. Murdoch writes in this regard:

> One may of course try to 'incarnate' the idea of perfection by saying to onself 'I want to write like Shakespeare' or 'I want to paint like Piero.' But of course one knows that Shakespeare and Piero, though almost gods, are not gods, and that one has got to do the thing oneself alone and differently, and that beyond the details of craft and criticism there is only the magnetic non-representable idea of the good which remains not 'empty' so much as mysterious.' (*SG*, p. 62)

Love reconciles us to our necessary fallibility as it introduces the idea of progress. Love involves an individual's acceptance of vulnerability, being determined by that which exceeds determination, coupled with a desire to bring her determinations into closer accordance with it – 'The lover who, nothing himself, lets other things be through him' (*SRR*, p. 270).

It is worthwhile considering an example in the form of a fictional incident from E. Annie Proulx's novel, *The Shipping News* (henceforth referred to as *SN*). The novel depicts the gradual transformation of its main character, Quoyle, who moves to Newfoundland, with his aunt and two daughters, to escape his dysfunctional life in the town of Mockingburg (obesity, unemployment, a deceased ex-wife and unhappy marriage and kidnapping by the ex-wife). He evolves as his conception of love evolves (reconciled to his obesity he is employed and engaged to be married). An incident that contributes to this evolution occurs early on in the novel when Quoyle accompanies a work colleague, Billy Pretty, to nearby Gaze Island, to 'touch up' Bill Pretty's father's grave – an annual ritual for the 70-year-old man. While Bill Pretty is weeding the grasses and painting the wooden headstone, he tells Quoyle stories he had heard about his father who died when Bill Pretty was only 15. As he watches and listens to Bill Pretty, Quoyle begins to engage his own reflections. He 'thought of his own father, wondered if the aunt still had his ashes. There had been no ceremony. Should they put up a marker? A faint sense of loss rose in him' (*SN*, p. 165).

This last sentence is suggestive because it may refer to more than one sense of loss. Quoyle may be aware of himself as having lost a father, for up until this point he had never acknowledged his father's death as a loss. It might also refer to Quoyle's sense of what he had lost in not having recognized his father as anything more than a parent. Quoyle had not had a sense of his father as a teller of stories, and so he was 'guessing at the dead man too late' (*SN*, p. 166). The loss is revealed to Quoyle in the context of Bill Pretty's life, precisely because Bill Pretty's life is cast by the meaningful relationship he has to the memory of his father. Quoyle effectively discerns in it a conception of 'son-ness' that is normative for him. Bill Pretty's annual ritual and rehearsed story-telling reveals to Quoyle the potential for his own life. We know from the character of Bill Pretty that he does not 'touch up' his father's grave because his father deserves it whereas some fathers might not; rather he does it because he is his father's son and this is how he honours his father, which is why he says to Quoyle that he will have to have his own inscription 'carved deep because there is nobody to paint me up every few years except some nephews and nieces down at St John's' (*SN*, p. 166).

So affected is Quoyle by Bill Pretty's ritual that it comes to serve as a reference point for his own reflections; he comes to appreciate his own life as limited in certain ways. Bill Pretty's ritual realizes (in the sense of making real) a different relationship between son and father, ramifying Quoyle's understanding of what it means to be 'son', 'father' and 'family'. Or it could be the case that Quoyle's response to Bill Pretty's ritual is motivated by a desire to think well of his father. Neither Quoyle nor the reader can ever really know that Quoyle is not self-deceived. It is significant that on his return to Killick-Claw, he does not erect a monument to his father or ask the aunt about the ashes, as if recognizing that it is not the details of Bill Pretty's ritual that constitute their significance but what these details exhibit or express. Quoyle is moved by the meaningful living-out of a father and son relationship, in the recognition that he might have had this kind of relationship with his own father but sadly did not. For Quoyle to take it up now as though he had done would be disingenuous on his part.

Towards the end of the novel, Quoyle receives a number of threats from a distant cousin who believes that he (Quoyle) has unfairly inherited the family estate. Quoyle visits his cousin, in anger, only to discover an old, physically and mentally ill, isolated man living in dire poverty. 'Quoyle could not shout at him, even for the witch-knots in his daughter's footsteps, even for the white dog that had terrified Bunny. Said "You don't need to do this." Which meant nothing. And he left' (*SN*, p. 265). Quoyle does not think of his cousin again until his friend Dennis mentions that it is time for the members of their community to provide the cousin with enough food and water for the winter. Quoyle feels suddenly guilty. 'He should have looked out for the wretched cousin the first time he saw him. Didn't think' (*SN*, p. 282). Shortly afterwards he arranges for the cousin to be hospitalized, but not without seeing him first.

Billy Pretty's ritual inspires and enlarges Quoyle's thought. It is an object of Quoyle's love because it imagines for him possibilities for his own subjectivity and relationships. Quoyle's learning is not instantaneous but slow and piecemeal, and requires further discipline on his part: he has good intentions but it takes time for him to realize them. This is in part because he does not simply 'latch on' to a concept of what it means to be a 'father', 'son' or 'cousin' and applies it in each subsequent case; rather this concept had to evolve with and through experience. Individuals communicate and learn their conceptual understanding through what they do, what happens to them and how they respond to what happens to them. This makes important not only dialogue but the sympathetic participation in the activities of each others' lives. For it is through such participation and dialogue that individuals learn and realize these alternative possibilities in the practice of their own lives.

Love has important ethical implications for interpersonal relationships. Unselfing entails that consciousness becomes less determined by the self and more available to reality. This reality that consciousness becomes determined by is principally made up of other individual selves who are also centres of meaning. They are 'fallen', subject to the egoistic fantasy mechanism of the psyche, inhabit different worlds, have occasional pedagogical encounters with the sublime, and find ways to articulate their perfectionist aspirations in what they say and do. The existence of others presents a transcendental limit to consciousness in the sense that consciousness will seek to marry its determination of discrete individuals with how they determine it. We are encouraged to appreciate the profound significance that others find in their lives and the reciprocal vulnerability that exists between us. Love generates endless responsibilities for others as they become, in a practical sense, a limit to our will. Bound by the beloved, we cannot anticipate what form our duties will take. The area of our obligation steadily increases, without promise of completion or relief. Even when we come to see 'what the situation requires' we can never be assured that we have got it right. When one finally makes a decision to keep the retarded child at home, ask the elderly relation to go away, leave one's family in order to do political work, one will never know whether one has behaved ethically or not. We are always left wondering, questioning, turned back towards the other in the spirit of dialogue and ever-present coexistence of competing truths.

Notes

Introduction

1. See Antonaccio and Schweiker 1996; O'Connor 1996; Antonaccio 2000; Nicol 2001 and Widdows 2005.
2. Some articles influential in the development of my interpretation of Murdoch include: Lloyd 1982; Blum 1986; Mulhall 1997; Kaalikoski 1997; Bowden 1998.
3. The Centre for Iris Murdoch Studies houses Murdoch's working library, Peter Conradi's working archive and a substantial collection of primary and secondary texts relating to the life and work of Iris Murdoch.
4. The first annual conference was held at Kingston University in 2004. See selection of papers from the conference, ed. Anne Rowe *Iris Murdoch: A Reassessment* (London: Palgrave/Macmillan, 2007).
5. See Byatt 1965, 1976; Todd 1979, 1984; Dipple 1982; Conradi 1986; Johnson 1987 and Nicol 2004.
6. Ironically, within these substantial exegetical works, the various connections between Murdoch's moral philosophy and the developments within contemporary moral philosophy that she contributes to are not discussed. In a book review of Maria Antonaccio's, *Picturing the Human: The Moral Thought of Iris Murdoch*, David McNaughton comments that her analysis of Murdoch's reflexive realism 'would have been helped by an awareness of McDowell's point that properties that cannot be grasped except by using concepts that make sense only to beings who share our form of life are nevertheless fully capable of being real and not in any way the constructs of our thought' (McNaughton 2002, p. 818).
7. Daniel Majdiak considers the influence of English romanticism on Murdoch's aesthetics and fiction, in particular her novels *The Time of the Angels* and *The Bell*. He argues that 'despite her criticism of Romanticism, she is in many ways a twentieth-century romanticist herself' (Majdiak 1972, p. 369). She makes a connection between 'sex and spirituality in ... thinking on love and death'(Majdiak 1972, p. 369). While I agree with much of what Majdiak says, I am more interested in the relationship between Murdoch's philosophy (not just her aesthetics and fiction) and the philosophy of romanticism.
8. Murdoch has been identified as an existentialist by some scholars and as a severe critic of existentialism by others.

9. Murdoch's location within the analytic tradition has eclipsed the uniqueness of her philosophical enterprise. She is well-versed in the analytic tradition and addresses the central arguments of its main proponents – directly referencing the texts of R.M. Hare, Stuart Hampshire, Gilbert Ryle and A.J. Ayer, and clearly opposing their shared moral psychology (*EM*, p. xii) – yet Murdoch remains an anomaly, drawing her philosophical inspiration from the classical philosophers of antiquity, continental existentialism and Christian mysticism, as well as enjoying a dual career as a philosopher and novelist.
10. Instead of interpreting Murdoch's moral philosophy through the lens of her Neoplatonism, I am interpreting her moral philosophy and Platonism through the lens of romantic thought. This makes sense if one realizes that early German romanticism is characterized as being the greatest revival of Platonic thought since the Renaissance. It is to these predecessors of Murdoch that I am drawing attention.
11. Murdoch does not mention the early German romantics and makes only a few brief references to the English romantics.
12. This emphasis on humility is reflected in Murdoch's austere reluctance to be prescriptive. She mentions learning Russian and potting plants as potential paths to the sublime, and she identifies mothers of large families as exemplifying humility, but does so only tentatively. She even works against her own intuitions by entertaining the possibility that 'the concentration camp guard can be a kindly father' (*SG*, p. 97).
13. Murdoch does not share the romantic confidence in *Bildung* because she takes seriously the doctrine of original sin and, consequently, is sceptical about the possibility of ever discovering a categorical imperative. Imperatives are, by definition, incomplete – it is their necessary incompleteness that defines our fallen human nature. If an ethical imperative can be derived from Murdoch's moral philosophy it is to be receptive, and 'cultivate' occasions for, 'the siege of the individual by concepts' (*SG*, p. 32). Not because it constitutes an end – this is the mistake the romantics made according to Murdoch – but because it facilitates a more truthful relationship with reality.
14. Plato is, for Murdoch, perhaps the best illustration of a 'great romantic' because he predates the 'distinctively aesthetic standpoint' established in the mid-eighteenth century and so is able to articulate a more profound appreciation of beauty and the significance of its impact on the human soul.
15. The early German romantics did not conceive of themselves as 'romantic'. The term, Beiser writes, 'was first applied to a later group of romantics only in 1805, and then it was used only satirically; it acquired a neutral connotation, more akin to contemporary meaning, only in the 1820s' (2003, p. 7).
16. For my characterization of this complex tradition, I rely on two distinct sources. First, I draw from the scholarship of Frederick C. Beiser (2003) for his analysis of early German romantics such as Schelling (1775–1845), Schleiermacher (1767–1834), Schlegel (1772–1829) and Novalis (Friedrich von Hardenburg) (1772–1801). Second, I draw from the scholarship of some contemporary philosophers, such as Richard Eldridge (2001), Russell B. Goodman (1990) and Nikolas

Kompridis (2006), who have produced contemporary reformulations of romantic thought in their interpretations of Ludwig Wittgenstein, Ralph Waldo Emerson and John Dewey.
17. The effect of romanticism has been existentialism (with its emphasis on absolute freedom) on the one hand and post-structuralism (with its emphasis on absolute determinism) on the other hand, both of which persuade 'by a sort of romantic provocation' rather than by virtue of their truth (*SG*, p. 47).
18. Murdoch identifies herself as fighting under the banner of Plato and writes that '[G.E.] Moore was in a way nearer the truth than he realized when he tried to say both that Good was *there* and that one could say nothing of what it essentially was' (*SG*, p. 42).
19. A way of differentiating between Plato, Murdoch and the romantics is in terms of what they see this transformation as consisting of.
20. Conradi, in his analysis of Murdoch's fiction, refers to this process as iconoclasm. Iconoclasm is defined as the destruction (and replacement) of 'religious' images, pictures and states of mind. The invocation of religion here highlights the mythical and imaginative status of these conceptual understandings, and our attachment to them – iconoclasm is difficult, risky and never entirely successful.
21. As Kompridis writes:

> We come to see agency as a matter of what we let ourselves be affected by rather than a matter of exercising control over what we encounter. This redirection of our inherited notions of agency from mastery to receptivity is what Emerson is up to when he inverts the unusual Kantian image of agency as spontaneous activity by making spontaneous receptivity primary. 'All I know is reception; I am and I have: but I do not get, and when I have fancied that I have gotten anything, I found I did not. (Kompridis 2006, p. 5)

22. For an excellent analysis of the role of newness in romantic thought, refer to Nikolas Kompridis' chapter, 'The Idea of a New Beginning', in Kompridis 2006, pp. 47–59.
23. Charles Larmore describes the romantic position as follows:

> Our highest aspiration ought not to be the stance of complete autonomy, in which we can stand back from our given social arrangements and appraise their merits in the light of historically transcendent principles. Our goal must instead be to acknowledge the concrete forms of life with which our strongest commitments are inextricably entwined and to seek our self-perfection within its limits. (Lamore 1996, p. 37)

24. For representation and discussion of the different uses made of literary examples by philosophy, see Eldridge 1989; Goldberg 1993; Nussbaum 1990; O'Neill 1989; Parker 1994; D.Z. Phillips 1999, Ch. 7; and Weston 2001.
25. Lloyd 1993, p. 172.

1 A Philosophy of the 'Third Way'

1. Maria Antonaccio represents Murdoch's ethics as a mediating position between two alternative lines of thought in contemporary and religious ethics:

    between those thinkers in the Kantian tradition who believe that the self constitutes its own world through its acts and choices apart from determination by the givens of its situation, and those thinkers descending from Hegel who believe that the aims and purposes of the self are in fact constituted by the givens of its natural, social, and historical existence in particular communities. (Antonaccio 2000, p. 8)

    Antonaccio does not use the third or middle way to distinguish Murdoch's *approach to* philosophy. William Hall refers to Murdoch as 'attempting to find and express what she describes in her book on Sartre as a philosophy of the "third way"' (Hall 1966, p. 308). He explains it in terms of the theory of the personality that engenders, namely, an individual who, neither conventional nor neurotic, is capable of accepting and growing from her own 'volcanic otherness' (Hall 1966, p. 309). My analysis resonates with Hall's, but gives a fuller account of Murdoch's philosophy of 'the third way', particularly with respect to the literary style of her philosophical writing and her interpretations of Plato and Kant.

2. The conceptual world of the reader, to quote Cora Diamond, is the reader's *life* with concepts: the 'doings and thinkings and understandings ... into which one's grasp of the concept enters' (Diamond 1988, p. 276). She goes on to say that a personalized use of a concept will express itself, then, by way of 'how it enters the ordering and articulating of our experience, how it contributes both to the ways we make sense of what we do and what happens to us, and to how we see the shape of our lives'(p. 268).

3. For an excellent discussion of Heidegger on the significance of 'humble everyday practices', see Hubert L. Dreyfus and Charles Spinosa, 'Further reflection on Heidegger, technology and the everyday', in Kompridis 2006, pp. 259–84.

4. Murdoch's conception of what is involved in reading a philosophical text and learning its philosophical concepts is critically influential for how she reads other philosophers and develops her own philosophical outlook. In the case of reading philosophers such as Plato, Kant and Sartre for example, Murdoch is interested in how their *thinking*, whose arguments are just a final accretion, illuminates discrepancies and certainties in human life. She is concerned to understand their theoretical specifications of 'the subject', 'reality' and 'good' by way of how these engage with 'ordinary' existence (familial relationships, education, domestic responsibilities). She acknowledges that she is putting Plato's 'argument into a modern context' (*MGM*, p. 511). Her conception is also evidenced by her keen interest in 'great metaphysical systems' and their ability to 'change the world' through their gradual effect upon cultural thought and ordinary consciousness (*MGM*, p. 267). She identifies Stuart Hampshire's 'man' as 'lurking behind'

political discourse and as 'the hero of almost every contemporary novel' (*SG*, p. 7). She refers to existentialism as a 'popular philosophy' capable of 'getting into the minds' of those who may be 'unconscious of its presence' (*SG*, p. 47). She argues that 'Hegel influenced Marx who influenced innumerable people. Derrida has influenced a generation of literary critics. A behaviourist moral philosophy may also contribute to creating an atmosphere' (*MGM*, p. 267).

5. Stephen Mulhall writes that her earlier work seems to

> achieve the structural clarity, the systematicity, the architectonic unity that one tends to expect of works avowedly part of the analytical philosophical tradition. To put it more bluntly: the trouble with *Metaphysics as a Guide to Morals* is that in general its sentences, its individual chapters and its overall structure appear extremely disorganized. (Mulhall 1997, p. 220)

6. *Elizabeth Costello* was published in 2003 to a mixed reception from the critics. The novel is selfconsciously literary tampering with its own genre in expected and unexpected ways. The most important of these is the novel's plot to its subject matter: events are not represented in chronological or psychological time, but are referred to in the context of the ideas that differentiate the novel's chapters or lessons such as 'realism', the problem of evil' and 'eros' as illustrations. Although the novel is about Elizabeth Costello – its main if not only character – the reader does not actually learn very much of the details of Elizabeth's life. Her character is not, however, a pretext for the questions of the novel; rather the novel re-inscribes the concept of 'character' by exploring Elizabeth's ideas about truth and the role of belief, realism within the bounds of human subjectivity, human inwardness, history and mortality, and the ethical significance of writing.

7. The relevance of Denham's article is evidenced by her three concluding theses described as 'pivotal to Murdoch's moral psychology' (Denham 2001, p. 618). These are (1) moral knowledge occurs within a first-person perspective; (2) moral judgements are, or should be, particularistic; and (3) in accurate moral vision, imaginative attention overcomes illusion and fantasy.

8. Green 2002, pp. 82–3.

9. Philosophy, conceived as an exercise in purified reason, is thought to escape the distorting influence of the imagination, transcending susceptibility to either misrepresentation or creative excess. Once the imagination is no longer viewed as a threat to 'truthfulness', the imperative for philosophy to transcend its limits dissipates.

10. She would have approved of Kearney's 'labyrinth of mirrors' as an apt metaphor for the imagination in postmodernism, for 'it produces only endless reproductions, copies of copies of copies where there is no longer any original'. I suspect that Murdoch would agree with Green that the concept of the imagination is under threat from such an image, but she would be more concerned about its implications.

11. The fundamental value which is lost, obscured, made not to be, by structuralist theory, is truth, language as truthful, where 'truthful' means faithful to, engaging intelligently and responsibly with, a reality which is beyond us. This is the

transcendental network, the border, wherein the interests and passions which unite us to the world are progressively woven into illusion or reality, a continuous working of consciousness. This is to speak of what is closest to us. 'Truth' is found in 'truthful endeavour', both words are needed in a just description of language. (*MGM*, p. 214)

12. Murdoch does not pretend to give 'a neutral logical analysis' (*SG*, p. 44).

2 Reading Murdoch: Literary Form and Philosophical Precedents

1. I am grateful to Mario Di Pailantonio (2006, p. 15) for formulation of this phrase.
2. Pornography could never be a sacrament (source of good energy) in Murdoch's view.
3. Commentators are attuned to the presence of irony in Murdoch's fiction. Gordon claims that Murdoch is reminiscent of Kierkeggard in her 'deeper ironies' and comments that 'In Murdochian tragicomedy, the success of this pilgrimage is usually incomplete and the final effect more or less ironic in consequence' (Gordon 1995, pp. 8, 10). Hague claims that Murdoch's belief that all 'language is essentially ironic' is necessary for appreciating the comic vision of her fiction (Hague 1984, p. 64). For it is the potential of language to lie and tell the truth, that creates situations that are comical. Hague concludes that 'Though the goal of the novel, for Murdoch, is as close a rendering of reality as is possible, the material it must use to create this reality is inherently laden with ironic, ambiguous and comic properties' (p. 66). If MacIntyre is right that Murdoch's novels are philosophy because they 'embody a theory about theories, a theory which is to some degree against all theory – including itself'(MacIntyre 1982, p. 15) then the claims about the irony of language could also apply to her philosophical writings.
4. A familiar term in literary criticism, irony has received increasing attention within philosophical literature over recent years, particularly in the analysis of Socrates and early German romanticism. See Nehamas 1998 (Ch. 2) and Rorty 1989.
5. For a discussion of the role of vigilance in John Dewey's philosophy, refer to Kestenbaum 2002.
6. Murdoch comments, partly in jest but also partly seriously, that 'possibly Heidegger is Lucifer in person' (*SG*, p. 72).
7. But she insists on keeping aesthetics and ethics distinct, highlighting how unlike other concepts the good really is – learning it, for example, is not straightforward; it is complex, takes time and moves on into ever-increasing depths.
8. I give a full account of attention in Chs 4 and 5.
9. Murdoch summarizes it as follows: 'The mind seeks reality and desires the good, which is a transcendent source of spiritual power, to which we are related through the idea of truth' (*MGM*, p. 56).

10. For an excellent discussion of Kant's attitude to his own inclination for metaphysical theorizing, see Kneller 2006.
11. It is noteworthy that Murdoch at first considered using a ritual instead of the now famous example of M and D (mother and daughter-in-law). She says, 'All sorts of different things would do for this example, and I was at first tempted to take a case of *ritual*, for instance a religious ritual wherein the inner consent appears to be the real act. Ritual: an outer framework which both occasions and identifies an inner event' (*SG*, p. 16).
12. Murdoch quotes Plato as saying that 'Good is what every soul pursues and for which it ventures everything, intuiting what it is, yet baffled and unable fully to apprehend its nature' (*Republic* 505E).

3 Romanticism Reconsidered

1. Philosophically, romanticism is associated with such historical figures as Samuel Taylor Coleridge (1772–1834), Johann Gottlieb Fichte (1762–1814), Friedrich von Hardenburg ('Novalis', 1772–1801), Friedrich Holderlin (1770–1843), Immanuel Kant (1724–1804), Jean-Jacques Rousseau (1712–78), Friedrich Wilhelm Joseph von Schelling (1775–1854), Friedrich Schiller (1759–1805) and Friedrich Schlegel (1771–1829). Its recent revival has been stimulated by the work of contemporary philosophers including Isaiah Berlin (1999), Frederick C. Beiser (2003), Stanley Cavell (1979), Richard Eldridge (2001), Manfred Frank (2004), Nikolas Kompridis (2006), Jane Kneller (2003) and Charles Taylor (1995). Their research has concentrated on: translation; the philosophical foundations of romanticism (Lacoue-Labarth and Nancy 1988; Frank 2004); the relationship between romanticism and postmodernism (Frank 2004); conceptions of the subject and subjectivity (Ameriks and Sturma 1995; Klemm and Zoller 1997); *Bildung* and modern education; and the relationship between romanticism and early American philosophy (Cavell 1979; Eldridge 2001).
2. I take this term from the title of Nikolas Kompridis's (2006, pp. 2–3) edited collection, *Philosophical Romanticism*. In the Introduction he delineates thirteen characteristics of philosophical romanticism, some of which are addressed in this chapter.
3. As Beiser observes,

> [t]he young romantics did *not* define themselves in terms of this concept. They never referred to themselves as *die Romantiker* or as *die romantische Schule*. The term was first applied to a later group of romantics only in 1805, and then it was used only satirically; it acquired a neutral connotation, more akin to the contemporary meaning, only in the 1820s. (Beiser 2003, p. 7)

4. I do not enlist Beiser's analysis of the metaphysical role of organism in early German romanticism, and do not agree with him that Kant's Copernican Revolution 'marks a fundamental break with the Platonic tradition' (Beiser 2003, p. 62).

5. Beiser argues that the 'romantics gave importance to beauty *because* of its moral and political dimensions' (2003, p. 40, emphasis added). It was 'the *ratio cognoscendi* – the criterion or means of knowledge – of the true and good' (2003, p. 40).
6. Beiser writes that 'the revival of interest in Plato in Germany began in the middle of the century, and then reached its zenith in the 1790s, the formative years for the romantic generation' (2003, p. 68); and later, 'It was in the 1780s that the Platonic renaissance truly began' (p. 68).
7. Beiser acknowledges that his analysis implies that Hegel's absolute idealism originated in the writings of Novalis, Schlegel, Holderlin and Schelling (2003, p. 66).
8. Duncan Heath and Judy Boreham write that

> By placing human subjectivity at the centre of our experience of 'reality' Kant implied that the world as it appears to the senses (pheneomena) and the world as it truly is (noumena) are distinct. German Romantics such as Holderlin, Novalis and Friedrich Schlegel, developed a philosophy of Being and an aesthetic which comprehended (without necessarily bridging) this gap. (1999, p. 82)

Stanley Cavell writes that romanticism is 'a poetic and philosophical response to an intellectual dilemma bequeathed to a new generation of European thinkers at Kant's death' (1979, p. 455); see also Cavell 1983. Russell B. Goodman writes that

> Kant's system is in fact part of the great humanizing movement described by Fryre in his *Study of English Romanticism*, in which European thought began to cast off 'an encyclopedic myth, derived mainly from the Bible', according to which God was the center of creativity, to work toward a new myth in which human creativity assumes a central place. (Goodman 1990, p. 12)

9. Beiser states, 'Kant's doctrine of the autonomy of art, his concept of an organism, his idea of the finality of nature, his definition of genius, and his suggestion that beauty is the symbol of morality were all crucial in one way or another for most young romantics' (2003, p. 79).
10. Eldridge aptly describes romanticism,

> in its simultaneous awareness of the situatedness and the unavoidability of its general reflections, in its simultaneous sense of the conditions and limits of general theorizing and refusal to scant our capacities for transcendence, in its resistance to closure while still seeking generality, and in its ambiguous alternations between traditional philosophical generalizing and traditional literary narration of the particular. (Eldridge 2001, p. 107)

11. Beiser's further argument is that the romantic conception of freedom results from a conception of nature as an organism which 'made humanity the telos of nature itself' (2003, p. 152). He writes that 'if the self is the highest expression of nature, then nature contracts to the limits of the self as the self expands to the whole of nature' (p. 152).

4 Resistance and Reconciliation

1. It is Plato's freedom from an 'aesthetics' discourse that enables a more profound appreciation of beauty and the significance of its impact on the human soul.
2. Of course, the scholarly and popular senses of romanticism are related – the caricature of romanticism has been informed by the scholarship (Isaiah Berlin, for example) that represents it as an inherently anti-rational movement.
3. I am indebted to Marije Altorf for pointing this out. See her unpublished manuscript, 'A Novelistic Philosopher: Murdoch on Imagination and Kant'.
4. Philosophers Margaret Holland and Lawrence Blum consider whether Murdoch's philosophy is susceptible to these kinds of criticisms in essays that are scheduled to appear in a forthcoming volume on Iris Murdoch.
5. See Chapter 2 of this book for a summary of Murdoch on the religious philosophies of Plato and Kant.
6. As Russell Goodman remarks in a footnote: 'Romanticism is in many ways an attempt to recover Greek and Roman ways of thinking and being' (Goodman 1990, p. 130).
7. Less typical, perhaps, are the philosophers identified by Murdoch as romantic: Rousseau, the early St Augustine, Schopenhauer, Nietzsche, Sartre and Simone Weil (*MGM*, pp. 132–3).
8. Conradi goes on to say that 'Religion, in Murdoch's view, is a recent invention. Spirituality and nihilism alike are ancient. It is to something like a Buddhist world-picture – in a sense a practical application of Plato's mysticism – that we now return' (Conradi 2001, p. 106). Maria Antonaccio argues that Murdoch's 'reflexive moral realism' occupies a 'third mediating position' in religious ethical debates between 'those who believe that the self has some capacity to transcend the commitments given by its situation, and those who appeal primarily to a narrative or tradition-based grounding for the self in its norms' (Antonaccio 2000, pp. 8, 10).
9. Beiser argues that

> The claim that the young romantics insisted that truth and value is a matter for the individual to decide fails to come to terms with the profound influence of Platonism on Holderlin, Schelling, Schleiermacher, Friedrich Schlegel, and Novalis. For all the importance that the romantics gave to individuality, they never ceased to hold that there are fundamental moral or natural laws that apply to everyone alike. Second, the romantics were also far from postmodernism in their striving and longing for unity and wholeness, their demand that we overcome the fundamental divisions of modern life. While the romantics recognized difference, and indeed celebrated it, they also believed that we should strive to reintegrate it within the wider wholes of state, society and nature. At least arguably, postmodernism begins with the claim that these divisions are a fait accompli and that there is no point striving to overcome them. Third, the romantics remained religious, and indeed even mystical. While their religion

had a pantheistic rather than theistic or deistic foundation, they never lost some of the crucial aspects of the religious attitude toward the world. It was indeed the self-conscious goal of Friedrich Schlegel, Novalis, Schelling, and Schleiermacher to revive this attitude, which is apparent in their call for a new religious mythology and bible for the modern world.' (Beiser 2003, p. 3)

10. Murdoch argues that 'The eclipse of death by creative suffering and the transformation of suffering and death in art are ways in which human beings make the intolerable tolerable, and Christian theology made use of these remedies long before the Romantic Movement' (*MGM*, p. 133).
11. Murdoch says of existentialist philosophy that it 'does so far pervade the scene that philosophers, many linguistic analysts for instance, who would not claim the name, do in fact work with existentialist concepts' (*SG*, p. 46).
12. Murdoch thinks that the exhilaration of existentialism is present in deconstruction, but that what invigorates it is the sheer 'impotence of the will and its lack of connection with the personality' (*SG*, p. 39). The thinking is: 'When I deliberate the die is already cast. Forces within me which are dark to me have already made the decision' (*SG*, p. 36).
13. It attributes 'to the individual an empty lonely freedom, a freedom, if he wishes, to "fly in the face of the facts"' (*SG*, p. 27). The individual is 'marooned upon a tiny island in the middle of a sea of scientific facts, and morality escaping from science only by a wild leap of the will' (*SG*, p. 27). The individual, who as agent, being on the cusp of acting, thinks, 'Here I stand alone, in total responsibility and freedom, and can only properly and responsibly do what is intelligible to me, what I can do with a clear intention' (*SG*, pp. 30–31).
14. Murdoch writes that 'What may be called the Kantian wing and the Surrealist wing of existentialism may be distinguished by the degree of their interest in reasons for action, which diminishes to nothing at the Surrealist end' (*SG*, p. 35).
15. She refers to her philosophy as offering 'a general metaphysical background', 'a *sketch* of a metaphysical theory, a kind of inconclusive non-dogmatic naturalism' and finally, 'a very tiny spark of insight, something with, as it were, a metaphysical position but no metaphysical form' (*SG*, pp. 42, 44, 73).
16. Other of Murdoch's formulations include: existentialism ignores that we are really like 'an obscure system of energy out of which choices and visible acts of will emerge at intervals in ways which are often unclear and often dependent on the condition of the system in between the moments of choice' (*SG*, p. 54), and

> We are anxiety-ridden animals. Our minds are continually active, fabricating an anxious, usually self-preoccupied, often falsifying *veil* which partially conceals the world. Our states of consciousness differ in quality, our fantasies and reveries are not trivial and unimportant, they are profoundly connected with our energies and our ability to choose and act. (*SG*, p. 84)

17. In respect of philosophical romanticism, Murdoch endorses its view that 'our sense of reality, and of the claims it makes on us, is inseparable from the creative

imagination' (Eldridge 2001, p. 3). Romanticism and Murdoch share a conception of morality as engaging 'the whole person and which may lead to specialized and esoteric vision and language' (*SG*, p. 43). Similarly, she defends her conception of art as having, *like romanticism*, an ideal morality in its background (*MGM*, p. 8).

18. It is telling in this regard that Murdoch does not criticize romanticism for evading the ideological by failing to heed the political and social determinations of imagination.
19. Eldridge 2001, p. 10.

5 Murdoch's Romantic Vision

1. Another commentator who appreciates the role of sublimity in Murdoch's thought is Peter Conradi. In his early work, *The Saint and the Artist: A Study of the Fiction of Iris Murdoch*, he dedicates an entire chapter to the role of the sublime in *The Bell* and *The Unicorn*, arguing that

   > The sublime is for Murdoch a central organizing metaphor, discernible in her plotting, her ethics, her aesthetics, and her use of ordeals by love and water. There is always more plot in her novels than the idea-play can use up, and this offers itself as a small hermeneutic sublime to the reader, who may feel, like one reviewer, that 'there is a central, large, and simple meaning which one has somehow just missed'. Such immersion of the philosophy in the data of action is paralleled by the immersion of the characters in the sublime of love. (Conradi 2001, p. 141)

2. 'Typically, it is thought, a Romantic poem will present an *isolated male protagonist* who reflects on *his life* in *strongly subjective terms* as he is halted *in a particular place*' (Eldridge 2001, p. 1).

3. Murdoch writes:

   > I have spoken of Shakespeare as being the greatest exponent of what I called, giving it too humble a name, that tolerance which we find also in great novelists. The pages of Shakespeare abound in free and eccentric personalities whose reality Shakespeare has apprehended and displayed as something quite separate from himself. He is the most invisible of writers, and in my sense of the word the most un-Romantic of writers. (*EM*, p. 275)

4. Conradi argues that the activity of swimming is Murdoch's image 'of a healing surrender to the mysterious supportive properties of the world, as well as its mysterious destructive properties' (2001, p. 137). Swimming imagines what it is like to allow one's consciousness to be determined by the undetermined, for 'both depend on one's willingness to surrender a rigid nervous attachment to the upright position and to feel, like Jake at the end of *Under the Net*, "like a fish which swims calmly in deep water ... the secure supporting pressure of my own life"' (p. 138).

5. I have in mind Rebecca Kukla's article 'Attention and blindness: objectivity and contingency in moral perception'. Kukla construes the Murdochian picture as *impersonalist*: Murdoch argues for excising the self in the interests of objective moral perception. Of the M and D example, Kukla writes that 'M is able to see better by withdrawing from the object of perception and suppressing her interests and idiosyncrasies. Her restraint cleans away the pollution of the self and her vision is thus classified' (Kukla 1998, p. 322). Kukla concludes that there is no room in the Murdochian picture 'for the self in its specificity to play a positive or productive role in the clarification of vision' (p. 323). In the article, Kukla critiques Murdoch's position through the sustained analysis of examples, arguing that at least some relevant moral perceptions are exclusively available to certain perspectives, engagements and social contexts. My point is that while Murdoch would agree with much of Kukla's argument, Kukla misconstrues what Murdoch means by 'unselfing' by giving inadequate consideration to its theoretical context. In other words, she focuses on Murdoch's philosophical moral psychology to the exclusion of her meta-ethics as evidenced by the following passage:

> The self, for Murdoch, is essentially corrupt and corrupting, and this is why it will pollute anything with which it allows itself to actively engage. Our self-interest runs so deep and is so inescapable that, if we do not abstract from our interests in vision, we will in effect see only our selves, and our gaze will be disrespectful and co-optive. (Kukla 1998, p. 331)

6. Simone Weil formulates the same point in terms of an analogy with reading. Individuals read others but rarely as others desire to be read. Individuals desire to be read as subjects, but we seldom see this because our perspectives are too self-centred and self-serving.

7. Ian McEwan's novels indicate a preoccupation with this dimension of human relationships. In *The Child in Time* McEwan narrates how a marriage is ruptured by the abduction of a young child; in *Saturday* he narrates how hope and familial love survive an, albeit explicable, outburst of arbitrary and irrational, violence perpetrated against them.

8. Carel, the main character of Murdoch's novel *The Time of Angels*, speaks to just how difficult it is to confront the formlessness of reality and dwell there; Carel's perspective is contrasted with that of his brother Marcus, who is represented by the novel as feigning such a confrontation. Carel states such stark truths as: 'Suppose the truth were awful, suppose it was just a black pit, or like birds huddled in the dust in a dark cupboard? Suppose only evil were real, only it was not evil since it had lost even its name? Who could face this?' (Murdoch 1966, p. 177); 'Any interpretation of the word is childish' (1966, p. 177); and finally,

> We do not know the truth because, as I told you, it something that cannot be endured. People will endlessly conceal from themselves that good is only good if one is good for nothing. The whole history of philosophy, the whole of theology, is this act of concealment. The old delusion ends, but there will be others of a different kind, angelic delusions which we cannot now imagine. One must be good for

nothing, without sense or reward, in the world of Jehovah and Leviathan, and that is why goodness is impossible for us human beings. It is not only impossible, it is not even imaginable, we cannot really name it, in our realm it is nonexistent. The concept is empty. (1966, p. 179)

It is not accidental to Carel's outlook and character that is felt to be, by his lover, daughter and brother, ethereal, impersonal and not-quite-human. His isolation intensifies over the course of the novel, ending in his suicide.

9. Murdoch writes that 'there is a special link between the concept of Good and the ideas of Death and Chance. (One might say that Chance is really a subdivision of Death. It is certainly our most effective *memento mori*)' (*SG*, p. 99).

10. Literature also depicts the process by which individuals confront their own internal barriers to seeing reality: fears, fantasies, memories, unresolved jealousies. It shows the process to be ongoing, slow, piecemeal and with many major setbacks. Literature engages with the contingent, complex and confusing messiness of human relationships and life.

11. Peta Bowden represents Murdoch as defending a form of altruism. For example, she paraphrases Murdoch as claiming that 'the object of attention is something so appreciated, so loved and cared about, that person can be prized away from their self-centered purposes and desires to possess or exploit it' (Bowden 1998, p. 64).

12. Stephen Mulhall writes that the significance of the void for Murdoch is that it raises the question of whether it reveals 'that the fundamental nature of reality is one from which Good is entirely absent' (1997, p. 238).

Bibliography

Note: For a comprehensive bibliography on Iris Murdoch, refer to *Iris Murdoch: A Descriptive and Annotated Secondary Bibliography*, comp. John Fletcher and Cheryl Bove (New York: Garland 1994).

1   Iris Murdoch

Philosophical works

Murdoch, I., 1952 'Nostalgia for the particular', *Proceedings of the Aristotelian Society*, 52 (June): 243–60.
—— 1953 *Sartre: Romantic Rationalist*. London: Penguin.
—— 1956 'Vision and choice in morality', *Proceedings of the Aristotelian Society* (suppl.), 30: 32–58.
—— 1959 'The sublime and the beautiful revisited', *Yale Review*, 49 (December): 247–71.
—— 1960 'Metaphysics and ethics', in D.F. Pears (ed.), *The Nature of Metaphysics*. London: Macmillan, pp. 99–123.
—— 1970 *The Sovereignty of Good*. London: Routledge & Kegan Paul.
—— 1977 *The Fire and the Sun: Why Plato Banished the Artists*. Oxford: Clarendon Press.
—— 1983 'Against dryness: a polemical sketch', in S. Hauerwas and A. MacIntyre (eds), *Revisions: Changing Perspectives in Moral Philosophy*, pp. 43–50.
—— 1986 *Ascastos: Two Platonic Dialogues*. New York: Viking Penguin and Notre Dame, IN. University of Notre Dame Press.
—— 1992 *Metaphysics as a Guide to Morals*. London: Chatto & Windus.

Edited collections and interviews

Conradi, Peter (ed.), 1997 *Existentialists and Mystics: Writings on Philosophy and Literature*. New York: Penguin Books.
Dooley, Gillian (ed.), 2003 *From a Tiny Corner in the House of Fiction: Conversations with Iris Murdoch*. Columbia, SC: University of South Carolina Press.

Novels

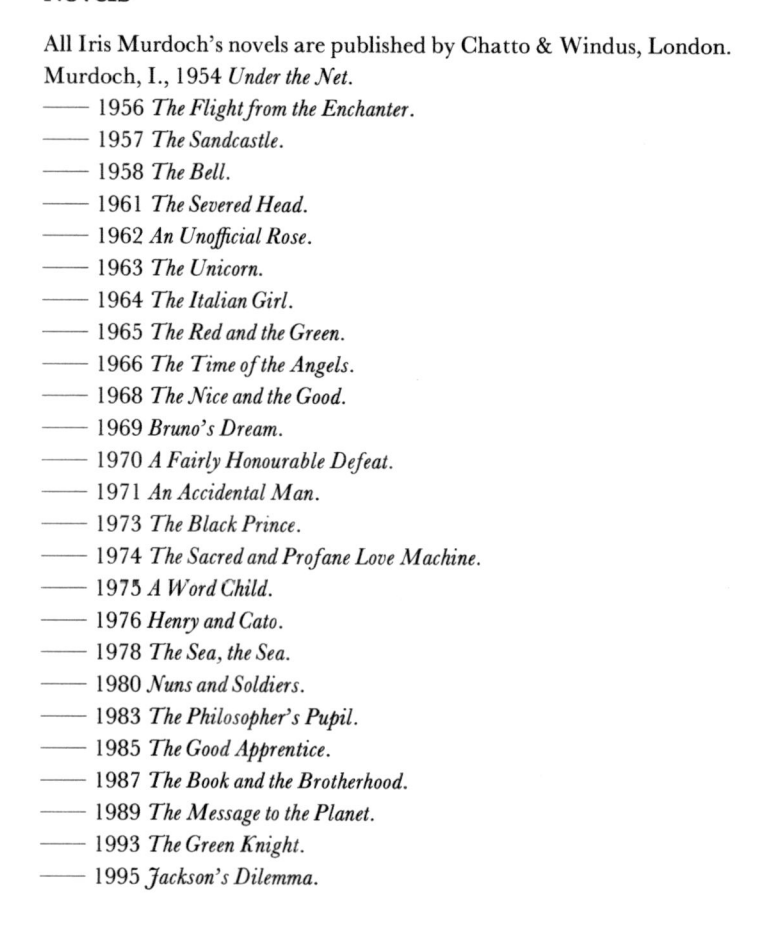

All Iris Murdoch's novels are published by Chatto & Windus, London.
Murdoch, I., 1954 *Under the Net*.
—— 1956 *The Flight from the Enchanter*.
—— 1957 *The Sandcastle*.
—— 1958 *The Bell*.
—— 1961 *The Severed Head*.
—— 1962 *An Unofficial Rose*.
—— 1963 *The Unicorn*.
—— 1964 *The Italian Girl*.
—— 1965 *The Red and the Green*.
—— 1966 *The Time of the Angels*.
—— 1968 *The Nice and the Good*.
—— 1969 *Bruno's Dream*.
—— 1970 *A Fairly Honourable Defeat*.
—— 1971 *An Accidental Man*.
—— 1973 *The Black Prince*.
—— 1974 *The Sacred and Profane Love Machine*.
—— 1975 *A Word Child*.
—— 1976 *Henry and Cato*.
—— 1978 *The Sea, the Sea*.
—— 1980 *Nuns and Soldiers*.
—— 1983 *The Philosopher's Pupil*.
—— 1985 *The Good Apprentice*.
—— 1987 *The Book and the Brotherhood*.
—— 1989 *The Message to the Planet*.
—— 1993 *The Green Knight*.
—— 1995 *Jackson's Dilemma*.

2 Articles and books on Iris Murdoch

Allen, D., 1974 'Two experiences of existence: Jean-Paul Sartre and Iris Murdoch'. *International Philosophical Quarterly*, 181–7.

Altorf, M., 2008 *Iris Murdoch and the Art of Imagining*. London: Continuum.

Antonaccio, M., 2000 *Picturing the Human: The Moral Thought of Iris Murdoch*. Oxford: Oxford University Press.

Antonaccio, M. and Schweiker, W. (eds), 1996 *Iris Murdoch and the Search for Human Goodness*. Chicago, IL: The University of Chicago Press.

Asiedu, F.B.A., 2002 'The elusive face of modern Platonism: Iris Murdoch and the ontological argument', *American Catholic Philosophical Quarterly*, 76.3: 393–410.

Bagnoli, C., 2003 'Respect and loving attention', *Canadian Journal of Philosophy*, 33.4: 483–516.

Bibliography

Bayley, J., 1998 *Iris: A Memoir of Iris Murdoch*. London: Duckworth.
—— 1999 *Iris and the Friends: A Year of Memories*. London: Duckworth.
Blum, L.A., 1994 *Moral Perception and Particularity*. Cambridge: Cambridge University Press.
Bowden, P., 1998 'Ethical attention: accumulating understandings', *European Journal of Philosophy*, 6.1: 59–77.
Burns, Elizabeth. 'Iris Murdoch and the nature of good', *Religious Studies*, 33: 303–13.
Byatt, A.S., 1965 *Degrees of Freedom: The Novels of Iris Murdoch*. London: Chatto & Windus.
—— 1976 *Iris Murdoch*. Harlow: Longman.
Coldstream, J., 2003 'Another perspective: Iris Murdoch's view of imagination, its connection with "quality of consciousness" and its role in moral education', *Prospero*, 9.3: 20–24.
Conradi, P.J., 1986 *Iris Murdoch: The Saint and the Artist*. Basingstoke: Macmillan.
—— 2001 *Iris Murdoch: A Life*. New York and London: Norton.
Denham, D.E., 2001 'Envisioning the good: Iris Murdoch's moral psychology', *Modern Fiction Studies*, 47.3: 602–29.
Dipple, E., 1982. *Iris Murdoch: Work for the Spirit*. London: Methuen.
Dunbar, S., 1978 'On art, morals and religion: some reflections on the work of Iris Murdoch', *Religious Studies*, 14: 515–24.
Gordon, D.J., 1995 *Iris Murdoch's Fables of Unselfing*. Columbia, MO: University of Missouri Press.
Hague, A., 1984 *Iris Murdoch's Comic Vision*. London and Toronto: Associated University Press.
Hall, W., 1966 ' "The third way": the novels of Iris Murdoch', *The Dallhouse Review*, 46.3: 306–18.
Hamilton, C., 1998 'Ethics and spirit', *Philosophical Investigations*, 21.4: 315–37.
Harcourt, E., 1998 'Mill's "sanctions", internalization and the self', *European Journal of Philosophy*, 6.3: 318–34.
Herman, D., 2001 'Introduction: approaches to Murdoch', *Modern Fiction Studies*, 47.3: 551–7.
Holland, M.G., 1996 'What's wrong with telling the truth? An analysis of gossip', *American Philosophical Quarterly*, 33.2: 197–209.
—— 1998 'Touching the weights: moral perception and attention', *International Philosophical Quarterly*, 38.3: 299–312.
—— forthcoming. 'Social convention and neurosis as obstacles to moral freedom', In J. Broakes (ed.), *Iris Murdoch, Philosopher*. Oxford: Oxford University Press.
Jasper, D., 1986 ' "And after Art ... nothing": Iris Murdoch and the possibility of a metaphysic', *Culture, Education and Society*, 40.2: 137–46.
Johnson, D., 1987 *Iris Murdoch*. Bloomington, IN: Indiana University Press.
Jones, J.A., 1998 'Teach us to see it: a retrieval of metaphysics in ethics', *Journal of Speculative Philosophy*, 12: 1–19.
Kaalikoski, K., 1997 'Replacing god: reflections on Iris Murdoch's metaphysics', *Journal of Speculative Philosophy*, 11.2: 143–60.

Kukla, R., 1998 'Attention and blindness: objectivity and contingency in moral perception', *Canadian Journal of Philosophy*, 28 (suppl.): 319–46.
Lloyd, G., 1982 'Iris Murdoch on the ethical significance of truth', *Philosophy and Literature*, 6: 62–75.
Loades, A., 1986 'Iris Murdoch: the vision of the good and the *via negativa*', *Culture, Education and Society*, 40.2: 147–54.
Majdiak, D., 1972 'Romanticism in the aesthetics of Iris Murdoch', *Texas Studies in Literature and Language*, 14.2: 359–75.
McDonough, S., 2000 'Iris Murdoch's notion of attention: seeing the moral life in teaching', *Philosophy of Education*, pp. 217–25.
Mulhall, S., 1997 'Constructing a hall of reflection: perfectionist edification in Iris Murdoch's *Metaphysics as a Guide to Morals*', *Philosophy*, 72: 219–39.
Nicol, B. 2001 *Iris Murdoch for Beginners*. New York: Writers and Readers.
—— 2004 *Iris Murdoch: The Retrospective Fiction*. New York: Pelgrave.
O'Connor, P.J., 1996 *To Love the Good: The Moral Philosophy of Iris Murdoch*. New York: Peter Lang.
Plant, B., 2003 'Ethics without exit: Levinas and Murdoch', *Philosophy and Literature*, 27.2: 456–70.
Pondrom, C.N., 1968 'Iris Murdoch: an existentialist?', *Comparative Literature Studies*, 5: 403–19.
Richter, D., 1999 'Virtue without theory', *Journal of Value Inquiry*, 33: 353–69.
Sage, L., 1977 'The pursuit of imperfection', *Critical Quarterly*, 19: 61–8.
Scanlan, M., 1977 'The machinery of pain: romantic suffering in three works of Iris Murdoch', *Renascence*, 29.2: 69–85.
Schauber, N., 2001 'Murdoch's morality: vision, will and rules', *Journal of Value Inquiry*, 35: 477–91.
Todd, R., 1979 *Iris Murdoch: The Shakespearian Interest*. London: Vision.
—— 1984 *Iris Murdoch*. London and New York: Methuen.
Vance, N. 1981 'Iris Murdoch's serious fun', *Theology*, 84.702: 420–27.
Warnock, M. (ed.), 1996 *Women Philosophers*. London: J.M. Dent/Orion.
Weldhen, M., 1986 'Ethics, identity and culture: some implications of the moral philosophy of Iris Murdoch', *Journal of Moral Education*, 15.2: 119–26.
Weston, M., 2001. *Philosophy, Literature and the Human Good*. London and New York: Routledge.
Widdows, H., 2005. *The Moral Vision of Iris Murdoch*. Aldershot: Ashgate.

3 Book reviews

Hepburn, R.W., 1978 'Review of *The Fire and the Sun: Why Plato Banished the Artists*, *Philosophical Quarterly*, 28: 269–70.
Holland, M., 1988 'Iris Murdoch and the search for human happiness', *Ethics*, 109.1: 179.
Kenny. A., 1971 'Luciferian moralists' review of *The Sovereignty of Good*, *The Listener* 85: 23.

Kleinig, J., 1971 Review of *The Sovereignty of Good*, *Australian Journal of Philosophy*, 49: 112–13.
Laverty, M., 1997 Review of Maria Antonaccio and William Schweiker (eds), *Iris Murdoch and the Search for Human Happiness*, *Australasian Journal of Philosophy*, 75.3: p. 132–3.
—— 2001 Review of John Bayley's *Iris: A Memoir of Iris Murdoch*, *Australasian Journal of Philosophy*, 79.1: p. 439.
MacIntyre, A., 1982 'Good for nothing', a review of Elizabeth Dipple's *Iris Murdoch: Work for the Spirit*, *London Review of Books*, 3.16: 15–16.
McNaughton, D., 2002 Review of M. Antonaccio's *Picturing the Human: The Moral Thought of Iris Murdoch*', *Ethics*, 112.4: 818.
Nussbaum, M., 1978 Review of *The Fire and the Sun: Why Plato Banished the Artists*, *Philosophy and Literature*, 2: 125–6.

4 Romanticism

Abrams, M.H., 1953 *The Mirror and the Lamp: Romantic Theory and the Critical Tradition*. New York, Oxford University Press.
Ameriks, K. and Sturma, D. (eds), 1995 *The Modern Subject: Conceptions of the Self in Classical German Philosophy*. New York: SUNY.
Babbitt, I., 1930 *Rousseau and Romanticism*. Boston, MA: Houghton Mifflin.
Bate, W.J., 1949 *From Classic to Romantic: Premises of Taste in Eighteenth-century England*. Cambridge, MA: Harvard University Press.
Behler, E,. 1990 *Irony and the Discourse of Modernity*. Seattle, WA: University of Washington Press.
—— 1993 *German Romantic Literary Theory*. Cambridge: Cambridge University Press.
Beiser, F.C., 2003 *The Romantic Imperative: The Concept of Early German Romanticism*. Cambridge, MA, and London, England: Harvard University Press.
Berlin, I., 1999 *The Roots of Romanticism*. Princeton, NJ: Princeton University Press.
Bernstein, J.M., 2006 'Poesy and the Arbitrariness of the Sign: Notes for a Critique of Jen Romanticism', in Kompridis (ed.), *Philosophical Romanticism*. London and New York: Routledge.
Bloom, H., 1973 *The Anxiety of Influence*. Oxford: Oxford University Press.
Bowie, A., 1990 *Aesthetics and Subjectivity: From Kant to Nietzsche*. Manchester and New York: Manchester University Press.
de Man, P., 1993 *Romanticism and Contemporary Criticism*. Baltimore, MD: Johns Hopkins University Press.
Eaves, M. and Michael F. (eds), 1986 *Romanticism and Contemporary Criticism*. Ithaca, NY: Cornell University Press.
Eichner, H., (ed.), 1972 *Romantic and its Cognates: The European History of a Word*. Toronto: University of Toronto Press.
Eldridge, R., 2001 *The Persistence of Romanticism: Essays in Philosophy and Literature*. Cambridge: Cambridge University Press.

Frank, M., 1997 'Subjectivity and individuality: survey of a problem', in D. Klemm and G. Zoller (eds), *Figuring the Self: Subject, Absolute and Others in Classical German Philosophy*, Albany, NY: State Unversity of New York Press, pp. 3–30.

—— 2004 *The Philosophical Foundations of Early German Romanticism*, trans. E. Millan-Zaibert. New York: State University of New York Press.

Furst, L.R. 1979 *The Contours of European Romanticism*. Lincoln, NB: University of Nebraska Press.

Goodman, R.B., 1990 *American Philosophy and the Romantic Tradition*. Cambridge: Cambridge University Press.

Hamilton, P., 2003 *Metaromanticism: Aesthetics, Literature and Theory*. Chicago, IL: Chicago University Press.

Heath, D. and Boreham, J., 1999 *Introducing Romanticism*. Duxford: Icon Books.

Henrich, D., 1992 *Aesthetic Judgement and the Moral Image of the World: Studies in Kant*. Stanford, CA: Stanford University Press.

—— 1997 'Self-consciousness and speculative thinking', in D. Klemm and G. Zoller (eds), *Figuring the Self: Subject, Absolute and Others in Classical German Philosophy*, Albany, NY: State Unversity of New York Press, pp. 99–133.

Izenberg, G.N., 1992 *Impossible Individuality: Romanticism, Revolution and the Origins of Modern Selfhood, 1787–1802*. Princeton, NJ: Princeton University Press.

Klemm, D.E. and Zoller, G. (eds), 1997 *Figuring the Self: Subject, Absolute, and Others in Classical German Philosophy*. New York: SUNY Press.

Kneller, J.E., 1997 'Romantic Conceptions of the Self in Holderlin and Novalis', in D. Klemm and G. Zoller (eds), *Figuring the Self: Subject, Absolute and Others in Classical German Philosophy*, Albany, NY: State Unversity of New York Press.

—— 2006 'Novalis' other way out', In N. Kompridis (ed.), *Philosophical Romanticism*. London and New York: Routledge.

Kohn, H., 1950 'Romanticism and the rise of German nationalism', *Review of Politics*, 12.4: 443–72.

Kompridis, N. (ed.), 2006 *Philosophical Romanticism*. London and New York: Routledge.

Kravitt, E., 1992 'Romanticism today', *Musical Quarterly*, 76.1: 93–109.

Lacoue-Labarthe, P. and Nancy, J.-L., 1988 *The Literary Absolute: The Theory of Literature in German Romanticism*, in trans. P. Barnard and C. Lester. New York: SUNY Press.

Langbaum, R., 1957 *The Poetry of Experience: The Dramatic Monologue in Modern Literary Tradition*. New York: Norton.

Larmore, C., 1996 *The Romantic Legacy*. New York: Columbia University Press.

Lockridge, L.S., 1989 *The Ethics of Romanticism*. Cambridge: Cambridge University Press.

Lovejoy, A.O., 1941 'The meaning of romanticism for the historian of ideas', *Journal of the History of Ideas*, 2: 257–78.

—— 1955 *Essays in the History of Ideas*. New York, George Braziller.

Phillips, D.Z., 2002 'Winch and romanticism', *Philosophy*, 77: 261–79.

Rush, F., 2006 'Irony and Romantic Subjectivity', in N. Kompridis (ed.), *Philosophical Romanticism*. London and New York: Routledge.

Weiskel, T., 1986 *The Romantic Sublime: Studies in the Structure and Psychology of Transcendence*. Baltimore, MD: Johns Hopkins University Press.

Winters, Y., 1974 *In Defense of Reason*. Denver, CO: University of Denver Press.
Yousef, N., 1999 'Wollstonecraft, Rousseau and the revision of romantic subjectivity', *Studies in Romanticism*, 38.4: 537–57.

5 Other works

Altieri, C., 1987 'From expressivist aesthetics to expressivist ethics', in A. Cascardi (ed.), *Literature and the Question of Philosophy*. Baltimore, MD: Johns Hopkins University Press.
Baldwin, A. and Hutton, S. (eds), 1994 *Platonism and the English Imagination*. Cambridge: Cambridge University Press.
Bates, J.A., 2004. *Hegel's Theory of Imagination*. New York: State University of New York Press.
Benhabib, S., 1992 *Situating the Self: Gender, Community and Postmodernism in Contemporary Ethics*. New York: Routledge.
Bernstein, J.A., 1980 *Shaftesbury, Rousseau and Kant: An Introduction to the Conflict Between Aesthetic and Moral Values in Modern Thought*. Rutherford, NJ: Fairleigh Dickenson University Press.
Cavell, S., 1979 *The Claim of Reason*. New York: Oxford University Press.
—— 1983 'Genteel responses to Kant in Emerson's "fate" and Coleridge's *biographia literaria*', *Raritan*, 3.2: 34–61.
Coetzee. J.M., 2003 *Elizabeth Costello*. New York: Viking.
Cordner, C., 1991 'F.R. Leavis and the moral in literature', In R. Freadman and L. Reinhardt (eds), *On Literary Theory and Philosophy: A Cross-Disciplinary Encounter*. Basingstoke: Macmillan.
—— 2002 *Ethical Encounter: The Depth of Moral Meaning*. New York: Pelgrave.
Crisp, R. and Slote, M. (eds), 1997 *Virtue Ethics*. Oxford: Oxford University Press.
Diamond, C., 1988 'Losing your concepts', *Ethics*, 98.2: 255–77.
—— 1991 *A Realistic Spirit: Wittgenstein, Philosophy and the Mind*. Cambridge, MA: MIT Press.
—— 2003 'The difficulty of reality and the difficulty of philosophy', *Partial Answers: Journal of Literature and the History of Ideas*, 1.2: 1–26.
di Pailantonio, M., 2006. 'Framing trials for past abuses through an "educative dialogue": recovering the formative role of conflict in a democracy', *Proceedings of the Annual Meeting of the Philosophy of Education Society*, pp. 59–67.
Eldridge, R. 1989 *On Moral Personhood. Philosophy, Literature, Criticism and Self-Understanding*. Chicago, IL: University of Chicago Press.
Gaita, R., 1991 *Good and Evil: An Absolute Conception*. Basingstoke: Macmillan.
—— 1999 *A Common Humanity: Thinking about Love, Truth and Justice*. Melbourne: Text.
Goldberg, S., 1993 *Agents and Lives: Moral Thinking in Literature*. Cambridge: Cambridge University Press.
Green, G., 2002 'The mirror, the lamp and the lens', retrieved 28 September, 2006, *Ars Disputandi*, 2, *ESPR Proceedings*: 75–86, http://www.ArsDisputandi.org

Grimshaw, J., 1986 *Feminist Philosophers: Women's Perspectives on Philosophical Traditions*. Worcester: Wheatsheaf.

Kant, I., 1952 *Critique of Judgement*, trans. J.C. Meredith. Oxford: Clarendon Press.

Kestenbaum, V., 2002 *The Grace and Severity of the Ideal: John Dewey and the Transcendent*. Chicago, IL: Chicago University Press.

Laverty, M., 2005 'The interplay of virtue and romantic ethics in Chang rae Lee's *A Gesture Life*', *Analecta Husserliana*, 85: pp. 191–205 A.T. Tymieniecka (ed.): pp. 191–205.

Lloyd, G., 1993 *Being in Time: Selves and Narrators in Philosophy and Literature*. London and New York: Routledge.

McDowell, J., 1979 'Vision and reason', *Monist*, 63.3.

—— 1983 'Aesthetic Value, Objectivity and the Fabric of the World', in E. Schaper (ed.), *Pleasure, Preference and Value: Studies in Philosophical Aesthetic*. Cambridge: Cambridge University Press.

Nehamas, A., 1998 *The Art of Living: Socratic Reflections from Plato to Foucault*. Berkeley, CA: University of California Press.

Nussbaum, M., 1990 *Love's Knowledge: Essays on Philosophy and Literature*. New York: Oxford University Press.

O'Neill, O., 1989 'The Power of Example', In O'Neill, *Constructions of Reason: Explorations of Kant's Practical Philosophy*. Cambridge: Cambridge Univesity Press.

Pétrement, S., 1976 *Simone Weil: A Life*. New York: Schocken Books.

Parker, D., 1994 *Ethics, Theory and the Novel*, Cambridge: Cambridge University Press.

Phillips, D.Z., 1999 'Nussbaum on Ethics and Literature', Ch. 7 in Phillips, *Philosophy's Cool Place*. Ithaca, NY: Cornell University Press.

Pippin, R., 2006 'On Becoming who One is (and Failing): Proust's Problematic Selves', in N. Kompridis (ed.), *Philosophical Romanticism*. London and New York: Routledge.

Platts, M., 1991 *Moral Realities: An Essay in Philosophical Psychology*. New York: Routledge.

Pouncey, P., 2005 *Rules for Old Men Waiting*. New York and London: Random House.

Proulx, A.E., 1993 *The Shipping News*. London: Fourth Estate.

Rorty, R., 1989 *Contingency, Irony and Solidarity*. Cambridge: Cambridge University Press.

Ruddick, S. 1995. *Maternal Thinking: Towards a Politics of Peace*. Boston, MA: Beacon Press.

Taylor, C., 1995 *Sources of the Self: The Making of Modern Identity*. Cambridge: Cambridge University Press.

Weston, 2001 *Philosophy, Literature and Human Good*. London and New York: Routledge.

Index

absolute 6, 32, 68–9, 71
absolutism 9
Adorno, Theodor W. 47
aesthetic 4, 8, 20, 48, 53, 61, 64–8, 71, 73, 98–9
agency 11–2, 20–2, 25, 38, 49, 55, 63, 65, 68, 70
Altorf, Marije 52, 118n.3
altruism 93, 98
Alzheimer's 1
ambiguity 3, 13, 19, 24, 28, 30, 32, 36–7, 40, 50, 56, 66, 68, 78, 83, 89, 105
analytic moral philosophy 4, 8, 84–5, 91
analytic philosophy 1, 3, 13, 49–50
Antonaccio, Maria 2, 42
art 6, 8, 10–11, 16, 20–1, 26, 29–30, 33–6, 38, 42–3, 45, 47–8, 52–3, 68–9, 71, 73–6, 79–80, 84–5, 96–8, 100–1, 103, 105–6
attention 7, 16, 20, 36, 48, 63, 80, 85, 104
axioms 48–9
Ayer, A.J. 80

barrier 9, 27, 52, 76, 78
Bayley, John 1, 89,
beauty 6, 24, 44, 59, 65–6, 68, 71, 73, 76, 79, 101, 105
becoming 11, 39–41, 55, 59, 61–2, 66, 70–1, 73, 76, 79
behaviorism 47
Beiser, Frederick C. 12, 14, 15, 58, 60, 63, 66, 69
Bernstein, J.M. 67
Bildung 7, 15, 64, 68, 71–2, 86, 111n.13
Blum, Lawrence 2
Bowden, Peta 2, 122n.11
Buddhism 26, 75

care ethics 2, 48
categorical imperative 78, 86, 111n. 13
Cavell, Stanley 16
chance 4–5, 15, 77, 84, 92, 95–6
child(ren) 6, 31, 44, 86, 93, 104
choice 9, 80–1, 106
Christ, Jesus 42, 83
Christianity 2, 22–3, 51, 75, 98
comedy 6, 10, 31, 88, 91
concepts and conceptual understanding 5–6, 9–12, 17, 19, 24–7, 29, 30, 32, 35, 38, 43–6, 51, 62, 68, 73, 87, 101–4, 107–8
contemplation 67
contingency 6, 11, 19, 30, 32, 35, 39, 41, 57, 59, 67, 69, 83, 91–2, 96–7, 105
Coetzee, J.M. 16, 22–4
Conradi, Peter 1–2, 20, 75, 92, 104–5, 112n.20, 120n.1
consciousness 3–7, 12, 15, 18–20, 24, 27–9, 34–5, 40, 42, 45, 48, 52–3, 55, 68, 76–9, 84, 87–8, 92–9, 101–8
Critique of Judgment 64–6, 89, 97

Diamond, Cora 2, 17, 102
death 4–8, 17, 35, 74, 76–7, 86, 88, 92–3, 95–6, 107
Denham, Ann 18, 26–7
Derrida, Jacques 16, 33, 47, 78, 80
Deconstruction 54, 91
determinism 3–4, 9, 33, 81–2, 74, 84
Doeuff, Michelle Le 16
domesticity 7, 13, 43–4, 85–6
Dostoevsky, Fyodor 80
dialogue 3–4, 12, 14, 19, 37–8, 45–9, 52, 54, 85, 104, 108–9
duty 48–9, 66, 72, 109

Eckhart, Meister 51
education 12, 14, 50, 52–6, 67, 70–2, 97
ego(ism) 4, 7, 14, 16, 19, 21, 33–5, 41, 45–6, 74–5, 77, 79, 81, 83, 87, 91, 98–9, 101, 105, 108
Eldridge, Richard 18, 59
Eliot, T.S. 89
elitism 15, 77–9, 84–5
energy 28–9, 40, 55–6, 62, 83, 97, 100, 105
Enlightenment 80,
ethics 2–3, 13, 15, 84
Existentialism 2–3, 9, 47–8, 69–70, 74–5, 80–2, 84, 91, 95
Existentialists and Mystics: Writings on Philosophy and Literature 1
evil 88, 101

fact/value distinction 49–50
faith 6, 9, 17, 30–1, 41, 51, 56–7, 66, 82–3, 88–9, 103
fallen (human condition) 5, 15, 32, 82, 87, 98, 108
fantasy 6, 10, 14, 19, 21, 25, 38, 46, 50–2, 56, 64, 71, 74, 77, 79, 81, 83, 88, 91–2, 97–100, 105, 108
fear 92, 94
feminism 2, 7, 13, 98
Fichte, Johann Gottlieb 69
finite 3, 22, 36, 57, 59, 61, 66–70, 87, 91
freedom 3, 6–7, 9, 11, 15, 33, 47, 64–5, 67–71, 73–4, 77, 81–2, 92, 95, 97
Friedrich, Casper David 94
Freud, Sigmund 38–9, 77, 83, 85, 98

Gadamer, Hans-Georg 89
Gaita, Raimond 2
gender 85
genius 21, 73, 77–80, 84
God 11, 29, 32, 43, 65, 83–4, 92, 95, 106
good(ness) 11–2, 15–16, 20, 32, 40, 43, 46, 51, 55–7, 64, 80, 83–4, 87–8, 95–7, 101, 106
Gorgias 4.
grace 6, 43, 53, 62, 66, 71, 75, 83, 88
Green, Garrett 18, 25–8

Hampshire, Stuart 80
Hare, R.M. 80
Hartman, Geoffrey 89
Hegel 34, 39, 80
Heidegger, Martin 33, 42, 78
heroic(ism) 7, 15, 54, 70, 73, 85–7, 91
Holderlin, Johann Christian Friedrich, 59
Holland, Margaret 11
Hume, David 42, 104
humility 7, 15, 42–3, 46, 63, 86–9, 95

imagination 4, 10, 12, 20, 25–6, 28–30, 53, 61, 64–5, 71, 73, 75–6, 82, 85, 89, 94, 96–97, 100, 103
icon(oclastic) 20, 28, 100, 112n.20
infinite 6–7, 15, 36, 59, 61, 67, 69–70, 87, 91, 101–2
irony 7, 12–5, 18, 38, 41–5, 62–3, 66, 68–70, 86–8, 115n.3

Kafka, Franz 41
Kant, Immanuel 3–8, 14–15, 18–19, 37, 42, 49–51, 53, 55–7, 64–8, 73–6, 83, 88–9, 94–5, 97–8, 103
kestrel 85, 102–103
Kierkeggard, Soren 39, 80, 82
Kneller, Jane 51
Kompridis, Nikolas 2, 10, 31
Kukla, Rebecca 121n.5

Larmore, Charles 10
language 9, 13, 17–8, 20, 26, 30–1, 33, 42, 48, 54, 67, 78, 87, 94, 106
learning 3, 5–7, 12, 20–1, 24, 29, 34, 38, 44–6, 50, 54–6, 71, 91, 101–2, 104–5, 108
lens 4, 25–7, 29, 58
literature 8, 16, 38, 54, 67, 87–9, 91–4, 96–7, 104, 105, 122n.10
love 11–2, 15–6, 21–2, 28, 32, 34, 44, 46, 54–5, 57, 62–3, 68, 71–2, 75, 82, 86–7, 89, 91–2, 95, 97, 101, 104–6, 108–9
Lloyd, Genevieve 16
Lucifer 42, 82

M and D 10, 85, 99–100, 102–3, 121n.5
McDowell, John 2

McTaggert, J.M.E.   18, 29, 43
Majdiak, Daniel   110n.7
Marxism   9, 47
meaning   4–6, 8, 11, 19–20, 25–6, 28, 35, 42, 44, 47, 64, 67, 78, 92–3, 103, 107–8
Meno   4.
metaphor   9, 19–20, 25, 29–30, 32, 37, 47, 51, 61, 94, 105
metaphysics   3, 9, 30, 32, 37, 42, 51–2, 56, 77, 82, 103
Metaphysics as a Guide to Morals   1, 11, 13–4, 29, 39, 46–8, 80.
Moore, G.E.   18, 29, 43, 48
moral(ity)   10–4, 22, 27, 34, 45–6, 48–9, 50, 53, 55–6, 76, 79–80, 85, 96, 105–6
Mulhall, Stephen   24, 35–6, 122n.12
myth   14–5, 51, 93–4

naivety   1, 9–10, 16, 40, 74, 102
nature   6–7, 15, 36, 38, 64–7, 70, 74–6, 78, 94–6
naturalism   29, 42
necessity   6–7, 11, 16, 30, 35, 50, 65, 67, 69–71, 74, 77, 82–3, 95, 97
new(ness)   10, 24, 61, 88–9, 100–1
New Testament   25
Nicol, Bran   2
nothing(ness)   4, 6, 74, 77, 84, 86–9, 96
Novalis   14, 59
Nussbaum, Martha   2

obedience   6, 11, 105
ontological argument   106
original sin   42, 82–3, 98

paradox(ical)   3, 7, 9, 22, 25, 57, 60–2, 91
perfection   15, 84, 105–6, 108
personality   15, 39, 83, 99, 105
Phillips, D.Z.   9, 90
philosophy   8, 13–4, 17–9, 29–42, 69, 78, 82–3
picture(s)   4, 32, 50–3, 57, 63, 78, 79, 89, 92–3, 98, 105
Pippin, Robert   60, 70, 71
Plato   7–8, 14–15, 17, 19, 37, 40, 47, 49–53, 55–7, 60–1, 73–4, 88

Platonic/ism   2–3, 9–10, 15, 45, 51, 60–2, 64, 73, 75, 95, 104
pluralism   12, 59, 66
post-structuralism   9, 47–8, 84
psyche   4, 6, 18–19, 77, 99, 108
Pouncey, Peter   16, 54–55
Proulx, E. Annie   16, 106–8

rationalists   9
realism   36, 83, 99.
reality   3–4, 8–10, 15, 18–20, 24–5, 28, 30, 32, 36, 49–52, 57, 61, 65–9, 71, 73, 76–7, 80–3, 87–9, 91–3, 96–103, 106, 108
reason   6, 9, 30, 32, 36, 60–1, 64, 67, 71, 75–6, 80, 83, 94–5, 99
receptivity   10, 31, 87, 93, 100
redemption   7, 9, 42–3, 46, 49–50, 62–3, 66, 71, 75–6, 84, 95
relativism   50, 80
religion   6, 13–14, 29–31, 42–4, 49–50, 57, 75–6, 82–4, 100
Republic   52
Ricoeur, Paul   16
ritual   107–8
Romanticism   2–4, 7–9, 11–15, 54, 58–79, 81, 84–6, 88–91
Rorty, Richard   16
Ruddick, Sarah   2
Rush, Fred   69

sacrament   40, 43–4, 55–6, 75, 97, 105
sado(masochism)   41, 64, 73, 85, 89, 95, 100
saint   86
Sartre, Jean-Paul   35, 80
Sartre: Romantic Rationalist   19
Schelling, Friedrich Wilhelm Joseph   14, 59
Schlegel, Karl Wilhelm Friedrich   14, 59, 67, 69
Schopenhauer, Arthur   47
scepticism   50, 61, 69, 104
science   6, 9, 28, 31–4, 43, 45, 38–40, 49, 64, 82, 106
Seel, Martin   60
Shakespeare, William   92, 106
sin   34, 43, 74, 82

Socrates 3–4, 42, 46, 86
Sophocles 79
The Sovereignty of Good xii, 1, 13–4, 29, 39, 46–8, 80, 89, 99, 102.
Steiner, George 34, 94–95, 101, 108
Steinkamp, Fiona 59
sublime 5–8, 15–16, 53–4, 65, 73, 75–6, 91, 94–8, 101, 103–5, 108
subjectivism 9
suffering 8, 11, 15, 22, 73–5, 77, 81, 83–4, 88, 91, 95

temperament 14, 34, 37, 38–41
tolerance 3, 92, 96
tragedy 6, 35, 91, 96–7
transcend(ent) 4, 7, 24, 29, 33–7, 41, 44, 50–1, 57, 62, 71, 73, 76, 78, 83–4, 88–9, 91–2, 100–3, 108
trust 6–7, 34, 93, 103–4
truth 5, 7, 9, 11, 15, 19, 21, 24–5, 27, 29, 32–6, 39–41, 44–6, 50–4, 56–7, 63, 68, 74, 78–9, 83, 86, 97, 101, 103

unity 4, 25, 34–6, 38, 40, 48, 61, 96, 98–9
unselfing 12, 52, 93, 95–6, 102, 105, 108

value 3, 12, 19–20, 33, 49–53, 56–7, 59, 64, 66, 70, 72–3, 77, 79–80, 83, 89, 105
vanity 84, 87, 102–3, 106
virtue 3, 7, 31, 60, 86–7, 97
virtuous peasant 3, 47, 85–6
void 4, 42, 97–8, 122n.12
vision 5, 10–2, 25–6, 29, 33, 36, 56, 67, 73, 78, 82, 91, 99
vulnerability 3, 5, 15, 24, 31, 81, 91, 93, 98, 106, 109

Widdows, Heather 2
will 29, 48, 80–1, 83, 109
wisdom 9, 61, 64, 86–7
Wittgenstein, Ludwig 40, 42, 46–7, 52